D1050239

THE GREAT ESCAPE
THE LONGEST TUNNEL

J940.547243 M561
Meserole, Mike.
The great escape

MID-CONTINENT PUBLIC LIBRARY
North Independence Branch
317 W. Highway 24
Independence, MO 64050

NI

WITHDRAWN
FROM THE RECORDS OF THE
MID-CONTINENT PUBLIC LIBRARY

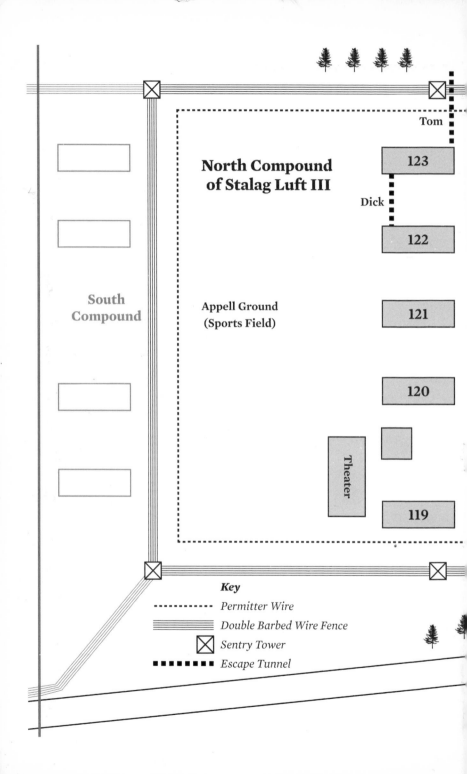

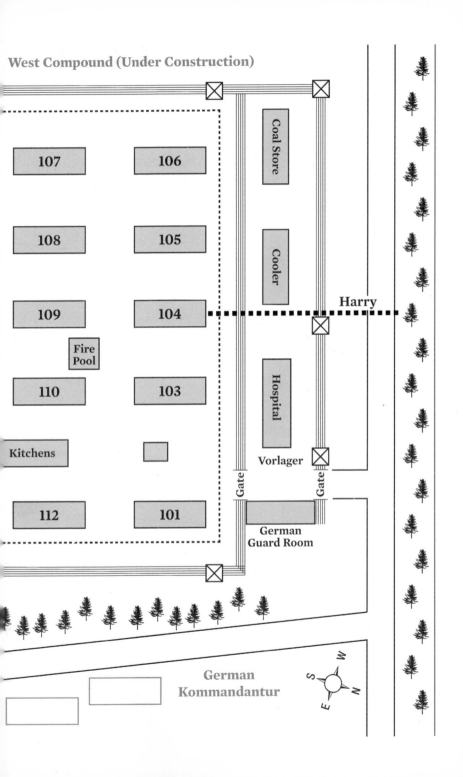

Guard tower at Stalag Luft III

THE GREAT ESCAPE
THE LONGEST TUNNEL

MIKE MESEROLE

STERLING

New York / London
www.sterlingpublishing.com/kids

MID-CONTINENT PUBLIC LIBRARY
North Independence Branch
317 W. Highway 24
Independence, MO 64050 **NI**

MID-CONTINENT PUBLIC LIBRARY - QU

3 0003 00421998 4

A FLYING POINT PRESS BOOK

It is our belief that any good story, whether fiction or non-fiction, requires dialog to give the reader a sense of immediacy. This is especially important when writing a book for young people. It is equally important to be faithful to historical accuracy. We feel strongly that any dialog included in a book should be based on sources such as journals and autobiographies. In no case should dialog be included that in any way distorts the facts of the story. We strive to publish books that live up to these standards.

Design: John T. Perry III and PlutoMedia
Front cover photograph: Major Johnny Dodge recaptured and escorted away by a large guard after jumping from a freight train.
Frontispiece photograph: Guard Tower
Interior photographs: Imperial War Museum (cover, frontispiece and pp 24, 54, 85, 93); Royal Air Force Museum (p. 25); United States Air Force Academy (pp. 12, 17, 108, 171)

STERLING and the distinctive Sterling logo are registered trademarks of Sterling Publishing Co., Inc.

Library of Congress Catalog-in-Publication Data Available

2 4 6 8 10 9 7 5 3 1

Published by Sterling Publishing Co., Inc.
387 Park Avenue South, New York, NY 10016
Copyright © 2008 by Mike Meserole
Map and drawings copyright © 2008 by John T. Perry III
Distributed in Canada by Sterling Publishing
c/o Canadian Manda Group, 165 Dufferin Street
Toronto, Ontario, Canada M6K 3H6
Distributed in the United Kingdom by GMC Distribution Services
Castle Place, 166 High Street, Lewes, East Sussex, England BN7 1XU
Distributed in Australia by Capricorn Link (Australia) Pty. Ltd.
P.O. Box 704, Windsor, NSW 2756, Australia

Printed in China
All rights reserved

Sterling ISBN 978-1-4027-5705-1

For information about custom editions, special sales, premium and corporate purchases, please contact Sterling Special Sales Department at 800-805-5489 or specialsales@sterlingpublishing.com.

To the Fifty

CONTENTS

1 It's an Officer's Duty to Escape   1

2 The New Big X   14

3 North Compound   19

4 The Tunnel King, the Ex-Con,
and the Penguins   33

5 Keeping a Secret   47

6 Digging Tunnels   53

7 The Fourth of July   58

8 High Stakes Chess   65

9 Tom Is Found   73

10 Tom's Revenge   81

11 The Yanks Move Out   88

12 Christmas Comes Early   95

13 Harry Reopens for Business   102

CONTENTS

14 Rubberneck Strikes   114

15 Harry Is Ready to Go   124

16 Tonight's the Night   134

17 Escape   154

18 The Cooler Is Full   168

19 Roundup and Reprisals   178

    EPILOGUE   195

    THE GREAT ESCAPERS   201

    BIBLIOGRAPHY   207

    INDEX   211

    ABOUT THE AUTHOR   226

THE GREAT ESCAPE
THE LONGEST TUNNEL

CHAPTER 1

IT'S AN OFFICER'S DUTY TO ESCAPE

AT THE BEGINNING OF WORLD WAR II THE only country able to make Nazi Germany back down was Great Britain.

The German war machine, under orders from dictator Adolf Hitler to "act brutally and show no pity," had rolled over Western Europe in just three months in 1940. By the time France surrendered that June, Hitler expected the British to be so scared they would give up without a fight.

Nothing doing. Energized by Prime Minister Winston Churchill's prediction that the coming Battle of Britain would be "their finest hour," the British fought on alone. And won.

In the first military campaign fought entirely in the air, the inexperienced and outnumbered Royal Air Force (RAF) defeated the previously unbeaten Luftwaffe in three grueling months. The RAF pilots, most of whom were boys in their early twenties, went up four to five times a day in their Hurricanes and Spitfires to take on the more seasoned Germans.

They had nerve. Flying at dizzying speeds of up to 370 miles an hour armed with four .303-caliber machine guns on each wing, most came back alive but many didn't. At work they operated in the shadow of sudden death. On the ground they let off steam by thumbing their noses at military convention. They dressed improperly and shaved irregularly. And when the battle was over Churchill said, "Never in the field of human conflict was so much owed by so many to so few."

After the Germans stopped throwing their fighter planes against the RAF during the day, they started sending their bombers over to terrorize London and other nonmilitary targets at night. The Blitz, as it was called, was a nine-month attempt to break civilian morale and force Britain to surrender. Despite 43,000 civilians killed and another 1,500 RAF casualties, that didn't work either.

The Luftwaffe gave up bombing Britain in May of 1941. A year later, RAF Bomber Command added to its regular attacks on German military and industrial targets by sending massive nighttime "thousand-bomber raids" against cities like Cologne, Hamburg, and Berlin. In January 1943 the Brits were joined by the U.S. Army Air Force, which preferred daylight bombing. German targets were now getting hit around the clock.

The increase in sorties meant that more Allied planes were being shot down over occupied Europe. The gauntlet of German air defense batteries stretching from Denmark in the north to the French-Swiss border in the south was ferocious.

While most downed flight crews were killed in action, the rest either survived their crashes or parachuted to safety. Very few, however, were able to avoid being rounded up by German military units or Home Guard patrols. When taken into custody, most newly minted prisoners of war heard the same confident declaration: *"Fuer dich ist der Krieg vorbei."* ("For you the war is over.")

Germany's first permanent prisoner of war camp for enemy airmen opened in July 1940 near the town of Barth on the Baltic coast. Stalag Luft I (Air Force Prison Camp I) was a drab little place surrounded by a nine-foot barbed wire fence. Twenty-one RAF officers moved in that first week. Less than two years later the inmate population of officers and crewmen had outgrown the camp's 800-bunk capacity.

The young British flyers proved to be anything but model prisoners. They complained about the shortage of food, refused to observe most military formalities, dressed like slobs, let their beards grow, and made sport of giving their captors a hard time at every opportunity.

They embraced the German word for prisoner of war (*kriegsgefangene*) by calling themselves "kriegies" and made up other less endearing names for everyone and everything else. Guards, for instance, were called "goons," a term taken from a British newspaper comic strip that depicted gooney cavemen as muscle-bound idiots. In that same vein, guard towers were "goon boxes" and badmouthing the enemy was "goon-baiting." Nosey guards who were specially trained to foil escape attempts were known as "ferrets." And the camp jail or punishment block was the "cooler."

Escape beckoned. Not everybody jumped at the chance because a fleeing prisoner might get shot. But it was always on their minds.

At first, security was lax and prisoners were allowed to leave camp for hour-long walking parties or soccer matches on the sports field which was a couple of hundred yards outside the fence. That first summer a few dozen kriegies sneaked off in search of a ferry to take them to neutral Sweden, but they were all quickly recaptured.

Getting caught after an escape was not a big problem. Prisoners of war were protected by the Geneva

Convention Agreement of 1929. The Agreement, signed by forty-one countries including Germany, prohibited reprisals against escaped POWs. It also required the recaptured prisoners be returned to the military rather than handed over to the police.

When the *Kommandant* at Barth cancelled the walking parties and beefed up the guard details on trips to the sports field, the kriegies started digging tunnels. Lots of them, all about six feet deep because of the shallow water table. By the summer of 1941, over thirty-five tunnels had been dug, but only four prisoners got out and only one made it to Sweden (and eventually back to London).

One of the first things that new Senior British Officer Harry "Wings" Day noticed when he arrived at Barth that July was that all escape activity was pretty much "every man for himself." There was no planning committee to organize the breakouts. In fact, in this growing community of grounded RAF hotshots, there didn't seem to be any adult supervision at all.

Day, a 43-year-old Wing Commander, was fighting in his second world war. In the first one, he had been a decorated officer with the Royal Marines. In this one, his reconnaissance plane had been shot down over France in October 1939. He was a POW of thirty-three months' standing and he had just been recaptured after leading an eighteen-man tunnel escape from a Luftwaffe transit camp in western Germany. If anyone could provide the leadership needed to organize these kids, it was Wings.

In time of war, it is every officer's duty to escape should he be taken prisoner. If there was an RAF code of conduct in prison camp, that law headed the list. The dream escape was the "home run," getting out and making it all the way back to London. But it rarely happened. The vast majority of escape attempts never made it out of camp, and those men lucky enough to actually get out were usually unlucky enough to get caught soon after.

The odds of gaining freedom were stacked against the prisoners and that was a drag on camp morale. Wings knew how to improve those odds: teamwork. Not everyone had the nerve to escape, but those who didn't want to break out themselves could contribute in other ways. The more prisoners involved, the better the chances for success, the bigger boost in camp morale.

Wings told the pilots, "for you the war is NOT over." Every man out forced the Germans to mobilize hundreds of soldiers, Home Guard, and local police. Mass breaks of five men or more multiplied the size of those manhunts substantially. A successful escape wasn't just making a home run. It could also be measured in tying up large numbers of Germans who would otherwise be aiding the enemy war effort.

Wings invented the X-Organization at Stalag Luft I. It took time to develop and didn't produce any spectacular escapes but it was an industry in the making. When Barth closed in March 1942 and the prisoners were transferred 300 miles south to a new Luftwaffe camp near Breslau, breaking out no longer meant flying solo. It was now a community effort.

Hermann Goering was a German WWI ace who ended the war with twenty-two confirmed shootdowns. Twenty-four years later, Goering was chief of the whole

Luftwaffe and the most powerful Nazi after Hitler. But unlike the rest of the Fuhrer's murderous inner circle, the sentimental Goering felt a chivalrous, "knights of the air" kinship with Allied flyers left over from a time when planes were made of canvas and wood.

Goering believed that enemy airmen deserved a prison camp where they could sit out the remainder of the war in relative comfort. That camp was Stalag Luft III, a new state-of-the-art facility in Lower Silesia. Carved out of a huge forest of scrub pines, it sat on the outskirts of Sagan, a town of 25,000 people about ninety miles southeast of Berlin.

Stalag Luft III opened its gates to 2,500 Allied airmen from prisons all over Germany in April 1943. The Luftwaffe boasted that the camp was escape proof and at first glance it certainly appeared to be.

Laid out in a rectangle measuring one mile by two miles, it consisted of a Center and East compound for prisoners and one for the German guards. The POW compounds were surrounded by two nine-foot-high barbed wire fences with overhangs that faced inward.

They were separated by an alley of dirt that was seven feet wide and filled with a thick and continuous coil of even more barbed wire.

Thirty feet in front of the inner fence was a shin-high warning wire that the German guards called the "line of death." Cross it without permission and a marksman in any of the ten 15-foot-high guard towers along the outer fence had orders to shoot. There was only one gate in and out of each compound and at night searchlights swept the grounds while guards with German shepherd dogs patrolled inside and outside the perimeter fences.

In the center of each compound were prefabricated wooden barracks, or huts, designed to hold a hundred men. There was also a small sports field, and three buildings holding a kitchen, a latrine, and a bathhouse.

There were only three ways out of a prison of war camp: over, under, or through the wire.

Climbing over was almost impossible and exposed the escaper to far too many dangers. Tunneling under was the best option but demanded organization. Also the Germans had two big things in their favor—microphones were buried under the fences to detect sounds of digging, and the ground underneath the camp was sandy and collapsed easily. Finally, going through the wire meant somehow bluffing your way out of the main gate or cutting through both the inner and outer fences.

The most dramatic escape from "escape-proof" Stalag Luft III came five months after the camp opened.

Ken Toft, an Irish pilot in the RAF, and Nick Nichols, a Californian in the RAF's American Eagle Squadron, had cased the East Compound fence for weeks and were convinced there was a blind spot halfway between two of the goon boxes on the east perimeter facing the woods. They figured at that point in the fence two men on their stomachs would be virtually invisible, screened from both towers by the dense coil of barbed wire between the inner and outer fences. Thus hidden, they could easily cut their way out.

Aware they would probably be killed by trigger-happy tower guards if their theory was incorrect, Toft and Nichols took the plan to Wings Day and his X-Organization assistants Jimmy Buckley and Roger

Bushell. Buckley was the "Big X," or operations boss, and Bushell was his number two. They checked out the blind spot and agreed it was worth a try.

Buckley plotted out a series of diversions that, if timed right, would distract all four goon boxes with a view of the escape route. Bushell ordered up false identity papers from the escape committee's forgery department and had the carpentry shop make a pair of homemade wire cutters and two fork-shaped pieces of wood to prop up the coiled barbed wire.

Colonel Friedrich von Lindeiner, Kommandant of Stalag Luft III

Two days later the daring escape went off without a hitch in broad daylight.

Unfortunately, Toft and Nichols were caught a few days later seventy miles north of Sagan. After being returned to Stalag Luft III, they were surprised when the camp's 61-year-old *Kommandant*, Colonel Friedrich von Lindeiner, invited them to his office.

Von Lindeiner was an ex-cavalry officer from the old school who had been decorated for valor during World War I. His posture was still ramrod straight and his uniform jacket and riding breeches were immaculately tailored. He wore the Iron Cross 1st Class on his left breast pocket.

He was aware of the RAF maxim that it was an officer's duty to try and escape and he respected it. As a token of his admiration for Toft and Nichols' daring escape from his camp, he presented them with a bottle of whiskey before sending them to the cooler for two weeks.

CHAPTER 2

THE NEW BIG X

THE GERMANS ELIMINATED THE BLIND SPOT along the East Compound fence but escape attempts continued. Over thirty tunnels had been unearthed in the six months since Stalag Luft III opened.

In early November German ferrets noticed fresh sand under one of the barracks. They discovered a tunnel, well built but poorly ventilated, that was about 300 feet long and less than seventy-five feet from the East Compound fence.

And this was *Kommandant* von Lindeiner's "escape-proof" prison. The *Kommandant* ordered the tunnel blown up. He also had all the known troublemakers in camp sent to an army officers' prison 200 miles away in Schubin. One hundred men were sent away in all, but the most important losses were escape committee leaders Wings Day and Jimmy Buckley, and a 48-year-old American-born British Major named John Bigelow Dodge.

Johnny Dodge was a tall, broad-shouldered adventurer with a big smile and a trim little mustache. His grandfather was Abraham Lincoln's first Ambassador to France and he was related to Britain's Prime Minister Winston Churchill by marriage.

As a prisoner of war "The Artful Dodger" never met an escape opportunity he didn't want to take. On the train carrying the expelled prisoners from Sagan to Schubin, he pulled up two floorboards in his boxcar and dropped himself through as the train slowed to enter a local station.

It was mid-morning and the guards on the back of the train saw him immediately. Seven jumped off and returned him to the idling train at gunpoint. Said Dodge with a wink after his recapture: "No harm in trying."

· · ·

The night before being shipped out of Stalag Luft III, Day and Buckley huddled with Roger Bushell. They handed over command of the X-Organization to Bushell and advised him to shut down all escape activity until the spring. Day's position as Senior British Officer in the compound would be taken by newly arrived Group Captain Herbert Massey.

The 32-year-old Bushell was from South Africa and as charming and dynamic as a squadron leader got. He stood a shade under six feet with an athlete's body that had grown gaunt in two and half years of captivity. A genius for organization and secrecy, he combined the fearlessness of a world-class downhill skier with the smarts of a Cambridge-educated lawyer, both of which he had been before the war.

He was fluent in French and German and had developed a flawless local accent on his frequent skiing visits to St. Moritz. A bad fall during a race in Canada almost cost him his right eye when the tip of his ski opened a gash between the eye socket and his nose. After getting stitched up, the injury left him with a slight droop in the

Squadron Leader and "Big X" Roger Bushell

eye that gave him a kind of sinister look. He learned to use that look to great effect when the occasion demanded it in court and later in the military.

Catching the flying bug at college, he joined the Royal Auxiliary and Reserve Volunteers after graduation in 1932. When the war came in 1939, he was asked to form the 92nd Squadron out of Tangmere Airfield south of London. The squadron was operational by the Battle of Dunkirk the following spring, and Bushell led his squadron of twelve inexperienced pilots into combat exactly twice—on the morning and afternoon of May 23.

He was shot down on his second mission over France and landed his mortally wounded Spitfire on a grassy field near Boulogne in territory supposedly still held by the French army. Seeing a motorcycle approach as he climbed out of his plane, Bushell lit a cigarette and waited to be picked up. Unfortunately, the motorcycle headed his way was German.

Bushell had a very good reason for hating the Germans. In an earlier escape attempt he had been sheltered by a Czechoslovakian family. These people were later executed by the Germans in a mass roundup to avenge a Gestapo leader's killing.

When Bushell was finally released from Gestapo custody in late August and delivered to Stalag Luft III in Sagan, he brought with him a cold hatred for the Germans.

He was also a marked man. When the Gestapo officer handed him over to *Kommandant* von Lindeiner, he said matter-of-factly, "Escape again, Mr. Bushell, and you will be shot."

CHAPTER 3

NORTH COMPOUND

WITH WINGS DAY, JIMMY BUCKLEY AND MOST of the other veteran escape artists banished from Stalag Luft III in November 1942, Roger Bushell was left to retool the X-Organization.

This job was made a lot easier in January when the sound of axes ringing in the woods north of camp brought word that the Germans were clearing land for a compound that would double the size of the prison complex.

The new North Compound was just what Bushell was looking for. Built from scratch and free of any underground tunnels, it offered him the opportunity to carry out a plan he'd been working on for months.

Addressing his top lieutenants—tunnel boss Wally Floody, head of security ("Big S") Bub Clark, and Floody's tunnel committee of Crump Ker-Ramsey, Johnny Marshall, and Johnny Bull—Bushell laid out his proposal with the care and directness of a prosecutor making his opening statement.

They would dig three tunnels simultaneously. That way, if the goons find one or even two, there will still be a third one well under way. No private tunnels will be allowed.

The three tunnels will be called Tom, Dick, and Harry and always be referred to by name. The word "tunnel" will *never* be used.

Tom, Dick, and Harry will be as well made as possible. They will each be thirty-feet deep with an underground railway for removing sand, a workshop for preparing the wooden framing to support the tunnel, and a station for pumping in fresh air.

Given the construction involved and the security

needed to keep the Germans in the dark, there will be no deadlines for completion. If the ferrets get overly suspicious about one tunnel, work will shut down on all three until the danger passes.

The directions and starting points of the three tunnels will be determined in advance.

When asked how many men he planned to break out, Bushell fixed the resolute gaze of his right eye on his fellow aviators.

"Everyone here in this room is living on borrowed time," he said. "By rights, we should all be dead. The only reason that God allowed us this extra ration of life is so we can make life hell for the Hun. Gentlemen, we will finish one of these tunnels. And I intend to send two hundred men through it in one night."

The escape committee let the audacity of the plan sink in for a few seconds before their startled faces broke into wide smiles and a feeling of confidence swept the room. They all agreed it would be impossible to hide three tunnels from the goons, but one, heck, they'd finish one for sure.

Next, Bushell rounded up his escape support specialists and told them exactly what he needed.

The volume of material was staggering. Two hundred fake passes from Tim Walenn's forgery department, which had no typewriters and would have to hand letter every pass. At least fifty suits of civilian clothes from tailor Tommy Guest and his crew. Two hundred compasses from industrial arts wizard Al Hake. A thousand maps from Des Plunkett, who had been an aerial surveyor before the war. And from Johnny Travis and his carpenters, the invention and construction of all the tunnel railways, air systems, and workshops.

There were some objections, but Bushell was ordering, not asking.

The following week SBO Massey went to see *Kommandant* von Lindeiner with an offer to send volunteers over to help prepare the new compound. The *Kommandant*, who prized cooperation between the Germans and their British guests, was delighted.

Soon small work parties of X-Organization members

were being marched over to assist German construction crews. They mainly stacked lumber and moved around bales of tarpaper. But what they were really doing was giving their future home a thorough going-over. They examined the foundations and structural integrity of all the barracks, paced off distances from each hut to the perimeter fence, and drew up an exact layout of the camp.

They also collected any pieces of lumber and metal, nails, electrical wiring, and half-empty bags of cement they could find and hid them in the empty huts for future use.

North Compound was roughly 350 yards square and penned in by the same nine-foot-high double fencing that enclosed East Compound. It was also surrounded by the same forest of miserable-looking scrub pine trees. The main gate at the northeast corner of the compound was the only entrance in or out.

Over the north wire was the *Vorlager*, or services facilities area. It held a small hospital, a coal shed, and a building that housed both the cooler and a storage room

A hut in the North Compound of Stalag Luft III

for food parcels from the Red Cross. To the east of camp, through a thin wedge of trees, was the *Kommandantur*, where the Germans had their garrison and administration offices.

Inside the compound were fifteen wooden barracks huts arranged in three rows of five, There was also a cookhouse, a fire pool, a washhouse, pit latrines, and the beginnings of a theater being built by the prisoners. A third of the compound was taken up by an unusually large sports field at the south end of the yard. The field doubled as the *appell* ground where roll calls were taken twice a day.

Each barracks consisted of eighteen bunk-rooms, a washroom, toilets, and a tiny kitchen. Fifteen of the bunk rooms could hold up to eight men comfortably with four double-decker bunks, a table for cards and eating, some chairs, storage cabinets, and a coal stove in one of the corners. The other three rooms had similar accommodations for two men each. The ranking officers in each hut bunked there.

Every bunk had a thin mattress stuffed with wood shavings and sawdust that lay on twelve removable bed

A drawing by a prisoner of a typical bunkroom in Stalag Luft III

boards. Those bed boards would be essential in shoring up the ceilings and walls in Tom, Dick, and Harry. With 126 bunks in each barracks there were more than 22,600 bed boards in the compound.

North Compound was finished in three months and opened on April Fool's Day. That morning 850 shabby and unshaven prisoners made the short walk to North Compound.

The move inspired a wave of escape fever.

Dozens of kriegies tried sneaking out the main gate in transport trucks, either hiding in the truck bed under big piles of pine branches or rolling underneath the truck and grabbing on to the chassis. They were all collared at the gate. Either by a goon with a pitchfork, who jabbed at each truckload of branches, or by *Oberfeldwebel* (Staff Sergeant) Hermann Glemnitz, the English-speaking senior noncommissioned officer in charge of security. Unlike most prison guards he was absolutely incorruptible and had a sense of humor that was very rare in the German military.

Glemnitz respected his prisoners and was respected and even liked in return. On the other hand, his second-in-command, *Unteroffizier* (Corporal) Karl Griese, was universally loathed by all, including his fellow ferrets. Nicknamed "Rubberneck" because of his unusually long neck and the odd way his head sat above it, Griese was every bit as incorruptible as his boss but never smiled. His passion for uncovering escape attempts, however, bordered on the pathological and that made him dangerous.

Rubberneck and the other ferrets stood out in their dark blue coveralls and caps. They had free run of the place from unlock in the morning until lockup at night. They could wander in and out of any barracks they wished without knocking, eavesdrop from hiding places under the floors and in the attics, and send anybody they regarded as suspicious to the cooler.

Each barracks was raised two feet off the ground so the ferrets could easily crawl underneath to check for the surest indicator of tunneling activity: sand.

. . .

27

In early April, several hundred Schubin inmates were brought back to Stalag Luft III where half were sent to the all-but-empty East camp and half to North. Among the new arrivals at North were old friends Wings Day and Johnny Dodge.

Dodge, a month away from his 49th birthday and the best storyteller and troublemaker of any room he walked into, used his elder statesman status to start an international affairs lecture and debating society that would evolve into the camp's most popular nighttime activity. He also became fast friends with Col. Jerry Sage, a newly arrived American paratrooper and hell-raiser, who was a spy for the Office of Strategic Services (OSS).

By April 11, Bushell and Floody had decided on the directions and starting points for the three tunnels. Tom and Dick would head west from the two barracks farthest away from the front gate, huts 123 and 122. That gave them the most warning time in the event of a surprise search.

Harry would go north underneath the *Vorlager* from Hut 104. Since this tunnel would have to be at least 100 feet longer than the other two, Bushell was counting on the practical Germans figuring a tunnel heading north made no sense.

Since all of the huts were raised two feet off the ground, there were only two ways to drop a vertical shaft straight down without it being seen: either by using the concrete drainage well under the washroom, or going through one of the solid brick foundations that supported the weight of the stoves in each of the barracks' 18 bunk-rooms.

The shaft down to Tom would start in a dark corner of the hallway behind the kitchen chimney in Hut 123. Dick would begin in the washroom of 122. And Harry would start under the stove in the last eight-man room at the north end of 104.

The trapdoors above those shafts were probably the single most important engineering job in the entire escape plan. The traps had to fit perfectly. Anything less would eventually be discovered by the ferrets.

Creating the traps fell to a very clever Polish RAF pilot named Minskewitz. For Tom, he chipped a two-foot-square slab out of the concrete floor and with the help of carpenter Johnny Travis replaced it with a thinner slab on top of a wooden frame that could be lifted out by inserting two thin wire hooks at the sides.

Dick's trap in Hut 122 was even more ingenious. The drain basin in the middle of the washroom floor was three-feet deep and covered by an 18-inch-square grate. Minskewitz removed the grate, mopped up the water in the basin, and cut out the left side of the basin wall exposing earth and sand. He then made a new concrete plate that could slide up and down to open and close the trap. Once the grate was replaced and a bucket of water tossed into the basin, no one would ever suspect there was a tunnel entry underneath.

The trap for Harry lay underneath a pot-bellied stove that stood on a concrete base of inlaid color tiles. Since the stove would have to always be red-hot to keep the ferrets away from it, the first problem was moving it to the side. That was solved by fashioning two wooden handles to lift the stove off its base and designing a simple extension to the stovepipe that led to the roof.

Next, Minskewitz chiseled the cement base down to the brick and replaced it with a wood-framed concrete trap door similar to the one he had made for Tom, only with hidden hinges for easier opening.

Manufacturing those traps, including the time it took for the new cement castings to dry, took about five days. The chiseling was noisy, but Minskewitz was protected by a network of kriegie lookouts, called stooges, who were arrayed around camp to signal the approach of any ferrets. If a German got too close, work was stopped until the all-clear sign was given.

The first three feet of the shafts for Tom and Harry had to be hacked out of solid brick foundations with a pickaxe before reaching bare earth. To drown out the noise of pickaxe biting into brick, Bub Clark set up diversions inside and outside first Hut 123 and then Hut 104.

The ferrets were used to passing by a barracks and hearing one or two kriegies hammering cooking pots and pans from used metal cans. So Clark multiplied the number of tin bashers by six and had a dozen guys inside banging away at metal cans.

Outside, there was an even louder racket. A chorus of British and American singers was recruited by Jerry Sage and led by choirmaster Johnny Dodge. The glee club's featured efforts included "I've Got Sixpence" and "I've Been Working on the Railroad." Each song was ably accompanied by an accordion and a rhythm section of barracks gardeners whacking the rocks around their vegetable patches with rakes.

CHAPTER 4

THE TUNNEL KING, THE EX-CON, AND THE PENGUINS

May–June 1943

ONE DAY, NOT LONG AFTER THE MOVE TO North Compound was completed, sign-up sheets appeared on barracks front doors. They were for spring sports leagues in soccer, cricket, and softball. Once word got out, however, that the sheets were also a secret way to enlist in the X-Organization, more kriegies scribbled in their names than the leagues could possibly handle.

One prisoner who declined to sign up was American

George Harsh, a quiet, white-haired 33-year-old tail gunner in the Royal Canadian Air Force and the only kriegie for whom life inside Stalag Luft III was a piece of cake.

Harsh was a convicted murderer who had done hard time on a Georgia chain gang.

Back in October 1928, he killed a drugstore clerk during a senseless stickup in Atlanta that involved five wealthy college kids looking for a thrill. The clerk fired first, wounding Harsh in the leg and accidentally shooting a second clerk in the head. But there was no denying that Harsh, a bored 17-year-old with a trust fund worth half a million dollars, had put three bullets into the chest of the clerk with the gun.

His capture and confession two weeks later made all the newspapers and the jury at his trial needed only 15 minutes to send him to the electric chair. The judge commuted his sentence to life on a chain gang, but wearing shackles and shoveling dirt all day in the company of rapists and homicidal maniacs was no life at all.

Some years later Harsh was suspected of helping in escape attempts, but nevertheless the prison foreman recommended him for a hospital orderly's job. There, Harsh came under the influence of a doctor who encouraged his interest in the healing arts by giving him a copy of the classic medical textbook, *Gray's Anatomy*, and letting him assist on operating room procedures.

On a late October night in 1940 an ice storm hit Atlanta, knocking down power lines and preventing the doctor from driving to the prison to operate on a convict with an inflamed appendix. Knowing the patient would die if the appendix weren't removed quickly, Harsh and the hospital's other orderly hung lanterns and flashlights over the operating table and went to work. Having seen the doctor perform the operation several times before, Harsh was able to successfully take out the appendix, sew up the incision, and dress the wound.

Within a month the patient was back shoveling with his work gang and Harsh was recommended for a full pardon by the doctor and the prison warden. The governor agreed and set Harsh free, saying he had served twelve years for taking a life and had now evened the score by saving one.

But there are no hero prison orderlies in the civilian world, only ex-cons. After six months of looking for a job, Harsh headed north to Canada. There he had no trouble getting a job hardly anyone wanted—tail gunner on an RCAF bomber. In October 1942, his plane was shot down over western France and he smashed several ribs hitting the ground hard in a parachute that was too small for him.

The only prisoner at Stalag Luft III who knew Harsh's story was fellow Canadian airman and tunnel king Wally Floody. After the move to North Compound, it occurred to Floody that "Big S" Bub Clark was going to need a full-time assistant for tunnel security to protect the existence and locations of Tom, Dick, and Harry from the Germans. Who better at keeping a secret in a prison camp than an ex-con? Plus Floody trusted Harsh.

"I want security people on top who will guard my back," he told Harsh. "We need you, George."

"You sure can sweet talk a guy," said Harsh. "How can I say no?"

Floody was a thin, 6-foot-2 Spitfire pilot with a full black beard and a passion for deep holes in the ground that seemed odd for a flyer. He was ten years younger than Harsh and had banged around the American West as a teenager before returning home to Northern Ontario to work for Lake Shore Mine, the second richest gold strike in the Western Hemisphere. He became one of the mine's most promising engineers.

Then came the war. Shot down over France in 1941, Floody had been digging escape tunnels since he was locked up in his first POW camp. In 1942 at Stalag Luft III he engineered an impressive 300-footer with two trapdoors under East Compound that the Germans discovered just before it was finished.

This time he really wanted to get out.

. . .

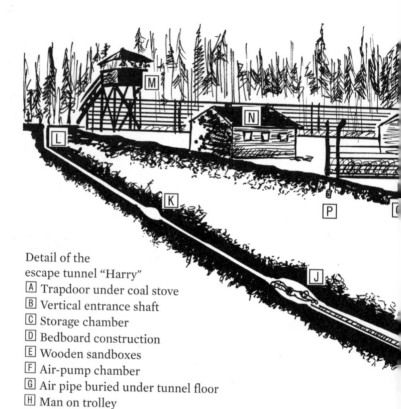

Detail of the
escape tunnel "Harry"

A Trapdoor under coal stove
B Vertical entrance shaft
C Storage chamber
D Bedboard construction
E Wooden sandboxes
F Air-pump chamber
G Air pipe buried under tunnel floor
H Man on trolley
I Wooden rails for trolley
J Halfway house #1 (Piccadilly Circus)
K Halfway house #2 (Leicester Square)
L Exit shaft
M Sentry tower
N Cooler
O Sick bay
P Sound detector under inner-barbed wire
Q Warning wire

Making the three trapdoors for Tom, Dick, and Harry and excavating down through the foundations completed the first phase of the construction project. Phase two was dropping vertical shafts under the traps to a depth of thirty feet. The shafts were two feet square and went that deep to evade the special noise detection microphones the Germans had buried three feet down at intervals along the entire perimeter fence.

At the base of each shaft three chambers were dug out to support the building of the tunnel. The first chamber was for holding sand to be sent back up the shaft for dispersal. The second was for a workshop to prepare the wood boards needed to line the tunnel. And the third was for an air pump, which would circulate fresh air and allow the diggers to work with the traps shut.

With digging under way on three fronts, sand quickly became Public Enemy No. 1. The gray topsoil that covered every inch of North Compound only went down six inches before giving way to a foul-smelling sand that was wet and bright yellow when freshly dug.

The sand presented two huge dangers. Below ground,

it was unstable and could collapse on the tunnelers at any time. Above ground, tons of it had to be hauled up and hidden from the ferrets who were constantly on the lookout for it.

Sand being sand, there was no way to eliminate the instability problem but it could be controlled by shoring up the shafts, chambers, and tunnels with wood boards. Luckily, wood boards were something that the new camp had plenty of in each barracks.

New Zealander Willy Williams, an eccentric 24-year-old Spitfire ace who shot down five Messerschmitts while wearing khaki shorts and sandals rather than service issue pants and boots, was the X-Organization's supply chief and head scrounger.

Asked by Floody to find solid bracing for the three shafts, Williams appropriated four bedpost frames from each hut. For everything else, he collected bed boards from beneath every mattress in every bunk in camp. Each bunk had twelve removable bed boards and each bed board was thirty inches long and six inches wide. With at least 126 bunks in each barracks there were more than

22,500 bed boards in the compound. The first levy was three boards from each bed, collected at the rate of several dozen a day.

Those bed boards determined the size of the tunnels. Cut in chamber workshops to insert tongue and groove, the boards were fitted together to line the walls and roofs of each tunnel. There was no need for nails or screws because the weight of the sand above held the framing firmly together. All shored up, the tunnels measured a snug two feet high and two feet wide—the size of a couch cushion. Not a problem. No one inside the wire at a German POW camp was overweight.

Cave-ins still happened. Floody was almost buried alive in Dick's shaft when one board snapped and several others came loose near the top of the ladder. The rupture set off an avalanche of heavy sand that came down so fast Wally couldn't scramble all the way up the ladder before the sand caught him by the waist five feet from the top. Crump Ker-Ramsey and Conk Canton, who had rocketed up the ladder before Floody, had to reach back down and pull him free.

The sound of an approaching collapse was unforgettable and always in the back of tunnelers' minds. It wasn't much, just a faint crack. But when you heard it, you either moved fast up the ladder or covered up down below and prayed someone was there to pull you out.

There wasn't very much talking underground. Mostly there was listening.

When Floody's East Compound tunnel was found, one of the kriegies overheard a confident Sergeant Glemnitz telling Captain Pieber, "They'll never get a tunnel out of here until they find a way to destroy the sand."

Destroying the sand fell to Hornblower Fanshawe. As sand dispersal chief, it was his job to make more than 230 tons of the yellow stuff disappear should all three tunnels be completed. Given sand's density, 230 tons would have filled a two-car garage.

Blocked from stashing the sand underneath the barracks because all the huts were raised two feet off the ground, the only alternative was to hide it in plain sight. Scatter it around the compound and mix it in with the dirt. But how do you carry the sand from the trapdoors above the tunnels to the prison yard outside without the Germans catching on?

Fanshawe then hit on an idea that was as brilliant as it was simple: trouser bags.

Hang two sand bags around a kriegie's neck, and lower the bags to knee level under his trousers, or pants. Each bag had three eyeholes at the bottom, through which a nail was inserted to hold in the sand. Each nail was attached to a long piece of string that ran back up each leg and through slits in the kriegie's pockets. Once out in the compound all the kriegie had to do was pull on the two strings releasing the nail and freeing the sand to pour down his legs and over his shoes.

The trouser bags were made by cutting the legs off a pair of woolen long johns, an item of clothing that was always in good supply thanks to the Red Cross. Filled with sand each bag weighed eight pounds.

When Fanshawe demonstrated his invention at a regular meeting of the X-Organization, an excited Bushell encouraged him to give it a try as soon as possible. "I already have," said Hornblower. "It works like a charm."

Mass production of the bags began immediately as the 200 kriegies who had volunteered for sand dispersal duty gleefully cut up their long johns.

A system was set up for moving the sand out of the tunnel and into the compound. Under the watchful eyes of security stooges, the sand carriers would line up in shifts to fill their bags, then proceed outside to a designated area of the compound, usually somewhere on the sports field, where they would pull their nails.

Waiting for them at the drop zone was dispersal coordinator Jerry Sage and up to forty roughnecks, mostly Americans, who were regularly engaged in unarmed combat drills or an intense game of football or rugby. Each sand carrier would walk into the middle of the match or mingle with the boisterous crowd surrounding it. He would then get jostled around as the sand fell out of his pants and wander off a bit dizzier for the experience.

Other more sedate dumping grounds were the kriegie

vegetable gardens that bordered each of the barracks huts, and the deep pit latrines.

Fanshawe's sand carriers, who all walked with a waddle when their trouser bags were full, were called penguins. Sage's roughnecks, who never let the dust settle around them wherever they went, were known as hooligans. And the sand they scattered around the compound in full view of the ferrets and the goon towers was made invisible, if not destroyed.

CHAPTER 5

KEEPING A SECRET

May–June 1943

A DUTY PILOT IN THE RAF WAS A FLYER WHO was assigned extra duties on a given day. Behind the wire at Stalag Luft III the "duty pilot" recorded all traffic in and out of the camp gate. The DP was the first line of the defense in Bub Clark's security network to protect not only Tom, Dick, and Harry, but also all support activities connected with Roger Bushell's plan to break 200 men out of North Compound.

The DPs rotated hourly and sat on a chair outside Hut 101 with runners on call to tail visitors or send status reports to X-Organization department heads. Each DP knew every German staff officer, guard, and ferret by sight, and entered the times of their arrivals and departures in a logbook.

They also used a Red Cross parcel box, a coal bucket and shovel set, and a small cement incinerator that stood nearby to indicate the current in-camp state of alert. The shovel in the bucket on the ground by the DP might mean the "honey wagon" was in camp to clean out the pit latrines (low alert). A shovel in the bucket sitting on top of the incinerator might mean two ferrets were inside (high alert).

Johnny Travis was a dapper Rhodesian who prided himself on being the cleanest shaven and best-dressed kriegie in camp. He had a theory that the ferrets equated pressed trousers and polished shoes with being a model prisoner and, sure enough, they never frisked him for contraband. Good thing, too, because under that well-tailored RAF jacket he wore Travis was a walking toolbox.

The room set aside as Hut 110's library was home base

for Travis's tin-bashing and woodworking shop. That's where Travis and ace carpenter Digger McIntosh spent hours making everything from chisels and screwdrivers to saws and wire cutters out of any metal objects Willy Williams could scrounge for them.

McIntosh spent the second half of April building a series of hidden walls in key rooms around camp where escape supplies could be concealed. The outer walls of all the prefabricated barracks huts were really double walls with four inches of space in between. McIntosh pulled the inner walls out another six inches to make a more substantial hideaway and added a trapdoor. The ferrets never suspected.

By mid-May, he was back with Travis in 110 to begin work on three hand-operated air pumps that would provide fresh air for the tunnelers down in Tom, Dick, and Harry.

Knowing that construction would be noisy, Bub Clark gave 110 the same coverage of lookout stooges the tunnel huts had. It didn't work. On the second day three ferrets crawled out from under Hut 103 and made for 110.

Caught by surprise, an urgent "Pack Up, Now!" signal was relayed to Travis.

Even with several stooges positioning themselves to slow down the ferrets' advance to the barracks, the carpenters had only about twelve seconds to stash their tools behind one fake wall, put the air pump they were working on behind another, and sweep the wood chips on the floor into a box that was stuffed in a bookshelf. When the ferrets burst through the door they found two kriegies hammering out baking dishes with an old pair of boots and two others beating on a nearby table like it was a set of bongo drums.

Close call.

The next day Roger Bushell ordered Jerry Sage and Johnny Dodge to organize an official camp choral club of no less than a hundred singers and hold practice every day outside the library window at 110. The singers had no idea they were being used as a diversion. In fact, one or two even leaned in the window and grumbled, "Will you guys keep it down, we're trying to sing out here."

Their industrial racket now drowned out by the thunderous serenade of the Sage and Dodge singers, Travis & Co. got back to making air pumps.

The key to the thing was the bellows, a flexible accordion-like air chamber that forced air through an opening when expanded and contracted. The bellows were made by cutting the bottoms off of two duffle bags, sewing the bags together, and reinforcing them on the inside with eight wire hoops.

Operating the pump was like sitting at a rowing machine: Pull the handle back to draw the air in and push the handle forward to force air up the tunnel.

Fresh air from above ground was sucked in through perforated bricks hidden in the hut foundations by Wally Floody's crew. Intake pipes made out of tin cans sent the air down to the pump room and then up the tunnel. There was also a separate exhaust pipe that funneled the foul tunnel air back up the shaft.

Thousands of tin cans were needed to make the air pipes and thousands were available. Every prisoner received a food parcel from the Red Cross each week that contained, among other necessities, a one-pound tin of

Klim powdered milk. (That's right, Klim is "milk" spelled backwards.)

Once the lines were tested, diggers could work below for extended periods of time with the trapdoors closed and greatly reduce the danger of discovery by the ferrets.

Kriegie electricians tapped into the camp's power grid but there was only enough wiring to reach the bottom of each shaft and light the three chambers. Tunnelers had to make do with fat lamps, which were English cigarette tins filled with boiled margarine that had been strained and cooled. A piece of pajama cord served as the wick. The lamp gave off some black fumes but the tunnel's exhaust system got rid of them.

Morning and afternoon *appells,* or roll calls, determined the start times of each shift as all prisoners had to be present at both head counts. The morning shift concentrated on digging and shoring up the tunnels, while the night shift attended to hauling up half a ton of sand for the penguins to disperse around the compound. The traps were closed during the morning shift but had to remain open at night, so security was tighter as it got dark.

CHAPTER 6

DIGGING TUNNELS

May–June 1943

DIGGING TUNNELS WAS NOT FOR WIMPS. IT was hard, filthy work in a hot confining space.

The only lighting was the candlepower of fat lamps hung every ten or twelve feet. And at any second a hundred pounds of smelly yellow sand could fall through the roof.

The tunnels were as wide as the inside of a bathtub and not quite as high as a tennis racket. That meant tunnelers, who worked in nothing more than long underwear, had to dig while lying on their stomachs or leaning on their elbows. When securing the walls and tunnel roof with wood boards they either twisted around on their sides or lay flat on their backs.

In previous tunnels under East Compound, moving fresh sand from the working face back to the base of the shaft was a slow and exhausting process. Diggers would fill a large pot with sand, crawl backwards with it to the shaft, empty the pot, then drag themselves back up to the face and repeat the trip.

For Tom, Dick, and Harry, chief engineer Wally Floody used his mining background to devise a much more efficient railway system to transport the sand and by the time the tunnels had pushed out twenty feet the tracks and trolleys were ready to go.

One of the trolleys used to transport sand out of the tunnels

Head carpenter Johnny Travis supervised the construction of the railway. He made rails from the wooden battens that lined the walls of every room. They were nailed into the floor of the tunnels a foot and a half apart.

The trolleys, which figured to get a lot of wear and tear, were constructed of beech bed boards. Designed by Travis and Bob Nelson, the wheels were made by gluing three disks together with the inside disk larger than the other two to form the flange that would keep the trolley on the rails. The axles rotated on wooden bearings greased with margarine.

With the railway system in place a second digger was added to each three-man shift to load sand on to the trolley and trade off when the first digger needed a break.

Digger No. 1 dug into the face of the tunnel with an empty powdered milk can or a metal trowel made in the carpentry shop. As the sand gathered around him he pushed it back past his hips where Digger No. 2 scooped it up and dumped it in the two sand boxes.

When both boxes were full, Digger No. 2 whacked the side of the trolley with his scooper and the Fourth Man hauled 200 pounds of sand slowly back to the shaft. He emptied the boxes into duffle bags in the sand dispersal chamber, put the boxes back on the trolley, and yanked the rope twice. Off went the trolley back up the tunnel. The Fourth Man was also occupied in the workshop chamber where he prepared the boards for shoring up the tunnel walls and roof. Those boards were also shipped to the face by trolley.

Over the course of a six-and-a-half-hour shift, diggers might trade places two or three times. If two small ones like Piglet Lamond and Geoff Cornish were paired, they could pivot and crawl over each other. Most, however, had to ride the trolley back to the base of the shaft and change up there. The new No. 1 Digger would then return to the face first, followed by the new Digger No. 2, who would rest his aching muscles while loading sand.

There was no lunch break mainly because a typical lunch in camp consisted of a slice of stale black bread and two potatoes. Not a very appetizing meal when mixed with sand and the sour taste of burnt margarine from the fat lamps. Water was available, however, in a covered pail at the base of the shaft.

The only contact the tunnelers had with life above ground was a warning tin containing three little pebbles that hung from the roof of the sand dispersal chamber. The tin was attached to a string that ran all the way up the shaft and through a small hole in the floor near the tunnel's trapdoor. If that string was yanked and the pebbles rattled around it meant that a ferret was snooping around the hut and everyone below should freeze.

The best diggers were of no particular size and came from ten different countries. Being a superior digger, however, didn't necessarily mean your sense of direction was perfect. Crump Ker-Ramsey had to schedule Canadians Hank Birkland and Scruffy Weir to follow each other in digging "Harry" because Birkland's tunneling hooked to the left and Weir's work veered to the right. Slotting one after the other was imperative to keeping "Harry" on course.

CHAPTER 7

THE FOURTH OF JULY

July 4, 1943

BY THE END OF JUNE A NEW COMPOUND was taking shape beyond the sports field fence south of camp.

A crew of about a hundred Russian workers and their machine gun-toting *Wehrmacht* chaperones had arrived on June 10 and started chopping down pines. In less than three weeks trucks had carried away enough tree trunks, branches, and other foliage to clear a campsite roughly half the size of North Compound.

In a meeting with von Lindeiner a few days after the

trees started falling, group captain Massey, the senior British officer, learned that the German High Command had ordered a new camp be built for Americans only.

"Surely that's not necessary" said Massey. "The Americans are our allies. We speak the same language and get along very well together."

"I think," said von Lindeiner, "that High Command and the Gestapo would agree with you. That is why you must be separated."

Time was now a factor. The target date for moving the Americans into South Compound was the end of August. If one of the three tunnels wasn't finished by then, no Yanks would be able to participate in the escape.

Bushell's reaction to the new development was quick and fair-minded. Calling an emergency meeting of the escape committee, he said that too many Americans had worked too hard in the tunnels and support factories to miss the breakout. He then proposed shutting down Dick and Harry and accelerating work on Tom, which was the furthest tunnel along at eighty feet.

The change of plans presented some new problems

but Wally Floody and his tunneling lieutenants thought they could manage them, as did sand dispersal chief Hornblower Fanshawe.

Floody said Tom had twenty-five feet to go to reach the wire and another 110 feet after that to make it safely inside the woods. By putting his fifteen best diggers on Tom and dividing them into three shifts, he figured the tunnel could advance ten feet per day barring complications.

Dick and Harry were closed and their trapdoors cemented shut after the last tunneling shift on June 15.

In the next two and half weeks a series of sand falls limited Tom's progress to about thirty feet, which put it about ten feet past the wire. The sand falls trapped Floody and his American partner Davy Jones several times but each was able to pull the other one free by his ankles. Every cave-in, however, took at least an hour to repair.

With the arrival of summer and the Americans' last two months at North Compound it occurred to Jerry Sage that a rip-roaring celebration of the Fourth of July was in order. And what better way to toast the Colonies' independence from the British in a POW camp where the Brits outnumbered the Yanks by 3-to-1 than getting everybody happily drunk on kriegie brew?

Kriegie brew was raisin wine with a heck of a kick. And like every other illegal activity at Stalag Luft III, where larceny, forgery, bribery, and deception were the norm, its manufacture was a British invention.

In order to "lay down a brew," as the process was called, a barracks mess of eight to twelve men had to save up a month's worth of sugar and raisins from their Red Cross parcels. That cache would then be emptied into a half-barrel of water with a fermented raisin begged from some other hut's brew to get things started. Once a brew was down, the fermentation cycle (converting the sugar to alcohol) lasted six weeks in cold weather, but only ten days in summer.

By the night before the big day dozens of gallons of liquid fireworks were standing in rows bottled in everything from washed out mustard jars to sand dispersal jugs. Fourth of July dawned sunny and warm but turned chaotic shortly after unlock at 7 A.M. when a parade of several hundred tipsy Americans invaded the British section of camp.

They were led by Uncle Sam (Sage in a red, white, and blue outfit and huge top hat), Paul Revere (Shorty Spire wearing a tri-cornered hat and riding two kriegies in a horse costume made in the tailoring shop), and a "Spirit of 1776" trio with piccolo, drum, and American flag. As Spire waved a wooden sword and hollered, "The Redcoats are coming! The Redcoats are Coming!" the rebellious Yanks raided every barracks and pulled every Brit from his bed.

Sage personally led the assault on Hut 110 where he barged into Roger Bushell's room saying, "Arise, the rebels approach! Don your red coat and fight like a man!" He and George Harsh then dragged Bushell out of his bunk and sat on him as the room filled with laughing Yanks and Brits. It was the first time anyone could remember seeing the Big X caught completely by surprise.

The parade then adjourned to the dispensing station in

the middle of camp where some 1,500 kriegies sipped brew out of shared tin cups and participated in a mass sing-along conducted by Johnny Dodge.

The Germans, who didn't know what to make of the celebration, tried to conduct morning *appell* as usual but it ended in a shambles. Pieber, realizing he would never get through the roll with such a boisterous and inebriated crowd, called off the count with a shrug of his shoulders and sent everyone back to barracks.

Except for the two clear-headed shifts that went below to work on Tom, the rest of the day was a blur of fun and games, picnicking on saved-up Red Cross parcel goodies, and the copious consumption of raisin wine.

At about 3:00 that afternoon, Sage's hooligans turned on their leader and tossed him into the fire pool at the center of camp. Wings Day, who always wore his full RAF uniform with World War I ribbons and commander's cap, then jumped in to rescue his American ally.

Within five minutes every senior officer in camp except Bushell had either been thrown into the pool or taken the plunge himself. Where was Roger? One step ahead, as usual. Figuring this might be a wasted day above ground, he had volunteered to join the tunneling shift down Tom.

By the time Bushell and the tunnelers emerged from Hut 123 just before the 5 o'clock roll call, North Compound was like a ghost town. From one side of camp to the other so many kriegies had conked out in their barracks that Pieber and his head counters went through each room and tallied up motionless bodies on bunks.

CHAPTER 8

HIGH STAKES CHESS

Mid-July to early-August 1943

SERGEANT GLEMNITZ WAS SURE THERE WAS a tunnel going out under the western fence.

After three months in North Compound the British and Americans had to be digging somewhere and the other three directions didn't make sense. The new American compound was being built to the south, the *Kommandantur* and German garrison lay to the east through a thin wedge of trees, and any tunnel going north would have to run an additional 200 feet or so to get under both the *Vorlager* and the road outside of camp to reach the woods.

Besides, the seismograph system the Germans had buried around the perimeter of North was picking up more below ground noise on the west side of camp than anywhere else.

There were three barracks along the west wire—Hut 106 in the northwest corner of camp, Hut 107 in the middle of the row, and Hut 123, which was the farthest barracks from the main gate. One of them was the origin of the tunnel Glemnitz was looking for and his money was on Hut 123.

The best way to find a tunnel at Stalag Luft III was to follow the sand. But the *Oberfeldwebel* and his ferrets had found very little of the yellow stuff despite their best efforts. He had to give the kriegies credit; up to now their security was better than his.

Then in mid-July one of the penguins dispersing sand from Tom got careless. He pulled the nails on his trouser bags at the edge of a crowd watching a volleyball game instead of wading in where he couldn't be seen. The sand was exposed for only a few seconds before it was covered up but Glemnitz, who was lurking nearby, saw it.

Next morning, ferrets armed with pickaxes and shovels came through the main gate and dug up every barracks vegetable garden looking for sand. They found a lot more than they should have.

At the same time tunnel security chief George Harsh noticed that the guards in the three goonboxes along the west fence were scanning the area with binoculars. He told Bushell they were obviously monitoring traffic in and out of huts 106, 107, and 123. Bushell responded by restricting all unnecessary movement through Hut 123 during the daily dispersal period between 5:30 and 9 P.M. He also asked Wally Valenta to have his goon tamers begin a whispering campaign that there was no tunnel and the kriegies were just trying to cause confusion.

So began the high stakes game of chess between Glemnitz and Bushell. Move and countermove with Tom's fate in the balance. Glemnitz attacking and Bushell protecting.

Glemnitz made his next move the following morning,

sending the loathsome Rubberneck and a dozen ferrets into camp to conduct a thorough search of Hut 106. It took four hours and the block looked like a hurricane had hit it when they were through. Hut 107 got the same treatment a day later, only that search lasted five hours.

As soon as the ferrets descended on 106, Bushell passed word to Hut 123 that all shifts down Tom were suspended until further notice and Minskewitz should seal Tom's trapdoor immediately. On the third day of Glemnitz's hut-by-hut search along the western fence the ferrets spent five hours tossing 123 and found nothing. Not even a false wall.

In subsequent days, barracks "Little S's," who scoured their huts for ferrets after morning and evening *appells* on the sports field, found a few hiding under the roofs and beneath the floors. And late one afternoon Hank Birkland, the Canadian jack-of-all-trades who knew a few things about hunting, spotted a ferret with binoculars in the woods beyond the north wire looking into camp from behind a "duck blind" of piled-up brush. He alerted Harsh and Bub Clark. After a hard look at the woods outside the west fence they noticed two more peeping ferret observation posts.

Bushell expected these increases in surveillance but he also had a timetable to consider. Prefabricated barracks were starting to rise on the new American compound.

Tom was reopened three days after the ransacking of huts 106, 107, and 123, and Wally Floody and his boys pushed ahead a record ten feet their first day back on the job. That amounted to over three tons of sand, more than the penguins could handle in one shift, especially with Hut 123 being watched closely by the goons.

Glemnitz kept up the pressure by springing a surprise head count at two o'clock one morning. He sent *Hauptmann* Pieber through every barracks in camp hoping to catch a few kriegies unaccounted for but came up empty-handed. Bushell was a step ahead of him. He had learned not to dig at night a year ago when a snap search in the wee hours of the morning at Stalag Luft I in Barth had caught several prisoners down a tunnel.

Later in the morning Glemnitz discovered large

deposits of fresh sand in the gardens around Hut 119 on the east side of camp. He hurried out of the compound and returned two hours later at the head of a column of a hundred soldiers, many of them with submachine guns. They were followed into camp by a truck carrying pickaxes and shovels and a staff car carrying the *Kommandant*, Security Officer Major Broili, and a very stern-looking cop who, given Broili's deference, must have been a big cheese from the Breslau Kripo.

Marching in quickly, the soldiers cut huts 106, 107, and 123 off from the rest of the camp and threw the kriegies out of all three barracks. The ferrets then tossed the huts for the second time in two weeks.

While that was going on, Glemnitz was outside Hut 123 drawing a line in the dirt that went the length of the barracks and halfway to the western fence. Pointing to the truck, he then ordered forty of the soldiers to grab a shovel or a pick and start digging a trench four feet deep and three feet wide.

When they were done a few hours later, Rubberneck and Adolf each pulled a five-foot metal rod out of the truck and jumped into the ditch. The two ferrets pushed their probes deep into the sand hoping to hit the roof of a tunnel, but they had no chance. The combined depth of the trench and the rods was only nine feet. Tom was another twenty-one feet down.

Bushell, Floody, and the rest of the escape committee watched the Germans from Hut 108 confident they would find nothing. Even when Rubberneck hit something solid and gave a shout, they showed no concern.

The Germans, however, got very excited. Glemnitz sent six soldiers into the trench to unearth whatever it was that Rubberneck had struck.

They found a big rock.

The Germans winced in disappointment while the three hundred or so kriegies who had gathered around the excavation site roared with glee.

A grim-faced Glemnitz gave up just before evening *appell* and ordered the trench filled. He left camp a beaten man but only for that day. He would be back and Bushell knew it.

Glemnitz was a bulldog. He had sunk his teeth into the

idea that there was a tunnel and he wasn't letting go until he found something.

At an escape committee meeting later that night, Clark recommended keeping Tom closed until things cooled off even if it meant that he and the other American would-be escapers might miss the boat. The Brits wouldn't hear of it. Digging on Tom would continue and the escape was still on for the end of August.

"But we can't let the damned Germans find any more sand," said Bushell, turning to Hornblower Fanshawe. "We're running out of places to hide it, Peter. What do you suggest?"

Fanshawe, who had been wrestling with the problem for a week, thought for another moment, then slapped his forehead with the palm of his right hand. "I don't know why I didn't think of this before, Roger," he said. "Why not put it down Dick?"

It was the obvious solution. Dick's seventy feet of empty tunnel could hold nearly twenty tons of sand and the best part was it was right next door.

CHAPTER 9

TOM IS FOUND

August–September 1943

THE MORNING AFTER THE GERMANS' TRENCH-
digging fiasco in front of Hut 123, Tom was reopened and
by that evening penguins were carrying sand to Dick's
trapdoor in the Hut 122 washroom.

Over the next week as Tom pushed out eight to nine
feet per day, Crump Ker-Ramsey and Johnny Bull began
refilling Dick with sand. They hauled it up to the face by
trolley and as the tunnel shrank little by little they sal-
vaged the wood shoring, the air pipeline, and the railway

tracks for use in Tom. Dick's workshop and air pump room would remain intact.

In the ongoing battle of wits between Glemnitz and Bushell, by early August everything seemed to be going Bushell's way. Tom had reached the edge of the woods, putting it just twenty feet from its planned exit point. And the ferrets hadn't found a speck of fresh sand anywhere in the compound.

Then trees started falling on both sides of the wire.

First, Glemnitz dealt a serious blow to escape committee security by sending soldiers in to cut down every remaining tree on the compound. Those trees had provided shade and a touch of privacy for each of the fifteen barracks and kept the camp from looking like a godforsaken wasteland. No more. And no more foliage to shield the huts from the prying eyes of ferrets, goonboxes, and snoops in the woods.

Second, the *Kommandant* had decided to expand again. This time to the west, where a work crew of half-starved Russian prisoners with axes began chopping down trees directly in front of Hut 123. Four days later, they were pulled off the job and sent somewhere else but not before they had rolled the edge of the forest back forty yards all along the outer fence. Now, instead of being twenty feet from completion, Tom had nearly 140 feet to go.

"Bloody funny coincidence," said Bushell. "But nothing has changed. We just pick up the pace."

Two weeks later, more bad news: Dick was full of sand. Bushell ruled out filling up the shaft because he needed the underground workshop and storage area. He also put Harry off limits because Harry was the back-up tunnel in case Tom was found. With sand pouring out of Tom at a record clip, getting rid of it was again a problem.

Dispersal coordinator Jerry Sage's two favorite dumping areas—the vegetable gardens around the barracks and the sports fields—were under tight surveillance by the ferrets. Plus penguin traffic in and out of Hut 123 was harder to camouflage without the cover of friendly trees.

Sage scaled back sand drops in gardens and on fields,

then he hit on another hiding place the ferrets would *never* suspect: Red Cross parcel boxes. They were the most common sight in a POW camp. Every kriegie had one under his bunk. Why not fill them with sand?

The next day all the Red Cross boxes in huts 101 and 103 by the main gate were filled with sand from Tom. Huts 101 and 103 got the nod because Glemnitz had just searched them and he tended to rotate his break-ins on a fairly reliable basis.

The dodge lasted five days. Glemnitz smelled trouble in Hut 103 and hit it with a snap search. Rummaging through a barracks room, one of the ferrets tried nudging a Red Cross box to the side with his foot but it didn't budge. Opening the box he discovered it was filled with sand as were all the boxes in the room. As were all the boxes in the barracks.

Glemnitz called in the heavy wagons and had them rumble around the area between 103 and the *Vorlager* fence in case there was a shallow tunnel underneath. There wasn't. The underhanded use of the boxes, however, led the *Kommandant* to suspend the distribution of

Red Cross parcels in North Compound until further notice.

By now it was late August and Bushell had a decision to make. Tom measured 285 feet long. Escape committee surveyors figured the tunnel was 140 feet clear of the outer fence but still forty feet short of the woods. The good news was that the vertical exit shaft would surface in darkness, well clear of the nightlights that bathed the nearest goonbox. Floody said it would take four days to dig up. The bad news was that sand dispersal was becoming a bigger problem every day, although Fanshawe said he'd think of some way to get rid of the stuff even if he and the penguins had to eat it.

Meanwhile, over the south fence, roofers and painters were finishing up the last of the barracks in the new American compound. Word from *Hauptman* (Captain) Hans Pieber, an engineer in civilian life, was that the Americans would be moved over in less than ten days.

After weighing all those factors, Bushell decided Tom had gone far enough and sent Minskewitz to seal its trap door. He then told Floody he could start digging up in three days, but first he wanted to try and convince Glemnitz there was no tunnel.

Sending for Sage, Bushell said he wanted fifty men, leaving in short intervals, to carry empty Red Cross boxes from Hut 103 to Hut 119. Sage got the caravan going about an hour later.

Ten minutes later Rubberneck realized something was afoot and sent for Glemnitz, who showed up at Hut 119 with a dozen guards and six ferrets. They evacuated the place, searched it for over three hours, and found nothing suspicious—except fifty empty Red Cross boxes.

That evening, one of Wally Valenta's "honest-faced" German speakers told Glemnitz in confidence that he knew nothing about a tunnel, but he *was* aware of a camp-wide attempt to have a laugh at the Germans' expense by running them all over the compound looking for something that didn't exist.

Everything he knew about the British and American prisoners told Glemnitz there was a tunnel. Still, in over four months he hadn't been able to find anything more than sand. Maybe he *was* having his leg pulled. Or the tunnel was going north, not west. Tunneling under the *Vorlager* was more work, but it was also a more clever choice. And the kriegies certainly were clever.

Two mornings later he decided to search huts 104 and 105 but changed his mind at the last minute and sent his men to Hut 123. As the barracks farthest away from the main gate, 123 was still the most obvious starting point for a tunnel and Glemnitz wanted to give it one last going over. If he came up empty again he'd give up and concentrate on the huts along the north fence.

The ferrets entered 123 just as the prisoners were returning from *appell*. Wally Floody, who had planned to go down Tom and start digging the exit shaft that morning, sent a runner over to Hut 110 to get Bushell and George Harsh. Looking on from just fifteen yards away in Hut 122, the three of them began a tense vigil that lasted two hours. Nobody spoke. Nobody had to. All that work. Would their luck hold?

It would not.

By 11:00 P.M. most of the Germans began filing out of the hut after another fruitless search. One of the last ones to leave, a ferret named Herman, was passing by the barracks kitchen when he stopped to randomly tap his metal probe across the bare concrete floor in the darkened corner by the chimney.

Listening for hollow sounds that would indicate an opening below the floor, he was startled when the point of his probe got stuck in the cement. Pulling it out, a small chunk of cement came out with it. That was odd, unless the cement was new. Getting down on his knees and taking out his flashlight for a closer look, Herman could detect the faint framing of a trapdoor.

The whoop of joy that followed his discovery was a dagger in the X-Organization's heart.

CHAPTER 10

TOM'S REVENGE

Early September 1943

HUT 123 SOUNDED LIKE THE VISITORS' LOCKER room after beating the home team for the championship. The visiting ferrets, having taken over the barracks to conduct a desperate last search for a tunnel, cheered their unexpected success while next door in Hut 122, the home standing escape committee cursed its fate in silence.

By the time the *Kommandant*'s staff car pulled up in front of 123, a large crowd of dejected prisoners had gathered around the hut trying their best to look unconcerned.

A triumphant Glemnitz greeted von Lindeiner and Broili as they got out of the car and led them inside where Rubberneck was waiting to smash in the trapdoor. When he was done, the four of them looked down on a thirty-foot shaft framed entirely in wood with a ladder anchored to one corner. Glemnitz gave a low, admiring whistle, then turned and motioned with his flashlight for Karl Pfelz.

Pfelz, a friendly little gray-haired ferret the kriegies called Charlie, was the only German with the nerve to crawl around underground. He took the light, climbed down the ladder, and disappeared into the darkness.

When he resurfaced a half-hour later, the euphoria Glemnitz felt with the discovery of the tunnel was tempered somewhat by Pfelz's assessment that it was well over 250 feet long and very close to being completed. He also said that the tunnel was so well shored up that the usual means of destruction—flooding it with water—would not be enough. This one would have to be blown up. Von Lindeiner told Broili to contact the Army engineers for a demolitions expert who could handle the job.

Later that afternoon Glemnitz put Hut 123 under 24-hour guard until the tunnel was destroyed and had Pieber re-assign the barracks's inhabitants to other blocks.

That night Bushell and Wings Day convened a three-hour meeting of the escape committee in Hut 110. Gloom filled the room. Not only had Tom been found and four and a half months of hard work wasted, but the Americans were being moved out in a few days and the compound was full of meddlesome ferrets. The two surviving tunnels would have to be closed until further notice, which meant that any mass escape was probably off until next spring.

No escapers were down in the dumps more than Mike Casey, who had been Tom's "trapfuhrer." Only twenty-five years old, he had just observed the fourth anniversary of his marriage, all but one month of it spent in German POW camps.

"It makes you wonder," Casey said to assistant tunnel chief Crump Ker-Ramsey, "whether we'll ever break one of these tunnels out."

"Don't let it get to you," said the Scotsman, who had been a prisoner since 1940. "By my count, Tom is only the ninety-eighth tunnel they've found."

The following morning von Lindeiner conducted a tour of Hut 123 for several high-ranking Gestapo officers up from Berlin as well as the Breslau Kripo chief.

Newspaper photographers were also on hand to snap pictures, including one of a smiling Rubberneck on the shaft ladder with his head sticking out of the old trap entrance. The other ferrets, none of whom liked Rubberneck much, couldn't remember the last time he looked so happy.

All the visitors marveled at the engineering skill of the prisoners but the Gestapo officers pointed out that the *Kommandant* had been very fortunate to find the tunnel before it could be used. They also said that they considered security at Stalag Luft III to be unprofessional and

The hated ferret Rubberneck after discovering Tom

warned that should there be a successful escape in the future, the Gestapo would deal harshly with both prisoners and the senior prison camp staff.

Von Lindeiner bristled at the arrogance of the officers but he knew it was no idle threat.

They were taking orders from Heinrich Himmler, the ruthless head of the RSHA, or Reich Security Office.

Himmler controlled the Gestapo (security police), Kripo (criminal police), the SS (political police), and the concentration camps. He also wanted to take charge of the prisoner of war camps but the military, particularly

Goering and the Luftwaffe, wouldn't hear of it. Blocked from extending his web of terror inside the gates of POW camps, he was determined to crack down on all escapers by having them turned over to the Gestapo, not the military, once they were caught. In Himmler's eyes escaping was not a prisoner's duty—it was a high crime against the state.

That afternoon a demolitions man arrived in camp to survey the tunnel and decide how much gelignite, or blasting gelatin, would be needed to blow it up. He needed two days to rig the explosives inside the tunnel and wire the charge to a detonator plunger box a safe distance away.

On the third day most of the kriegies in camp turned out for Tom's execution. Pushed back by gun-toting guards, they formed a semi-circle from Hut 107 to Hut 122 to the western end of the sports field.

Expecting a controlled underground explosion, the crowd got a major fireworks display instead. More of a demolitions amateur than an expert, the sapper had packed the tunnel with twice as much gelignite as the job required.

So when he pushed down the plunger he triggered a blast that not only took out the entire tunnel but roared up the shaft and blew half of Hut 123's roof off. The barracks also lurched forward as it was knocked from its moorings.

Momentarily stunned by the violence of the eruption, the crowd of POWs recovered quickly and erupted in its own explosion of laughter and abuse that sent the hapless sapper home in disgrace.

It took workmen more than two weeks to make Hut 123 habitable again.

CHAPTER 11

THE YANKS MOVE OUT

September–October 1943

THE AFTERNOON AFTER TOM WAS DISCOVERED
Bushell called a meeting at the new kriegie-built theater
in the southeast corner of camp. He began his pep talk by
reminding the audience that the whole reason for
building three tunnels was that one or two might be
found. The Germans had accidentally come across Tom,
but there were still two tunnels left that they didn't know
about.

He announced that Dick and Harry would be sealed
until further notice but that planning would continue for

a 200-man breakout. In the meantime, he wanted them to wear glum faces and "let the goons think that they have beaten us."

On September 8, two columns of armed guards marched the Americans out of North Compound to their new quarters just over the fence in South Compound. In the fast-growing Allied bombing campaign over Europe the Brits flew the night missions while the Americans handled the more numerous and hazardous daylight attacks. More American planes involved meant more shoot downs and, if they survived, more captured U.S. airmen. The number of Yanks at North Compound had quadrupled from 200 to over 800 in just five months.

The Germans had wised up since North Compound opened in March. This time around they prohibited the Americans from lending a hand in building the camp; they chopped down every tree in the yard ahead of time, disposed of every loose piece of lumber or construction material before moving day, and didn't put up with any "escape fever" shenanigans during the first week.

Fortunately, the Yanks weren't searched very closely as they entered the new camp. Sneaking in contraband was no problem, from a radio and digging tools to maps and forgery equipment.

The Americans would be missed, but the handful who served in British Commonwealth uniforms, like new "Big S" George Harsh and goon-tamer George Webster, remained behind.

For the last several weeks Bushell had directed Valenta's men to spread the word to their German contacts that it was the Americans not the British who were obsessed with escaping. And the biggest troublemaker was Bub Clark, the fresh-faced West Point grad.

Setting Clark up was a nasty thing to do, but Bushell, the *real* escape-obsessed troublemaker, was more concerned about Harry than Bub. If the whispering campaign worked, the Germans would put their best security people in South Compound to watch Clark and the Americans and ease up on the RAF officers in North. The Brits could then resume work on their third and last tunnel.

Meanwhile, Bushell had insulated himself from suspicion by staying in the background where Glemnitz and his ferrets couldn't see him pulling the X-Organization strings. He also made a point of appearing in a comedy that opened the new theater the same week Tom was found.

Glemnitz and von Lindeiner both saw the play and fell for the con. Discussing security assignments the next day, the *Kommandant* asked his sergeant who he thought was the most dangerous prisoner in camp.

"Without a doubt it is Colonel Clark," said Glemnitz.

"Not Squadron Leader Bushell? asked von Lindeiner.

"I believed so once, Herr *Kommandant,*" said Glemnitz. "But the Squadron Leader has become very quiet. He is more interested these days in the theater."

A week later, the Americans were transferred to South Compound and Glemnitz went with them.

Rubberneck became the new security chief at North and his promotion to sergeant made him even more obnoxious, if that was possible, to both prisoners and ferrets. His first order of business was to forbid any more fraternization between ferrets and the kriegies.

Bushell sent tunnelers back down Dick and Harry on September 13. He re-sealed the traps two days later when Harsh and Fanshawe told him that Rubberneck was driving his ferrets hard and it was still too dangerous to disperse sand around camp.

With the Russians returning to the woods over the west fence to resume clearing trees for another compound, Bushell downgraded Dick to a workshop and storage area only and designated Harry as the escape tunnel. Harry would be closed until January, while Dick would be opened daily so that Johnny Travis could send one of his carpenters down to work on the bed boards. The boards needed to be cut so that they would fit tongue and groove when it came time to resume digging and shoring up Harry.

Elsewhere in camp, it was full speed ahead in the escape support factories manufacturing the forged passes and identity cards, the maps and compasses, the civilian clothes and German uniforms, and the security net of stooges to protect them from the ferrets.

With the cold weather coming, the cricket and soccer

Some of the forged documents used by the escapers

leagues rushed to get their schedules completed on the sports field. As prisoners spent more time indoors, correspondence courses resumed for those wishing to further their education, especially those escapers who wanted to learn German. And the theater became a hub of activity, showing the first batch of English and American films and staging several kriegie-produced dramas and musical revues.

Von Lindeiner, who was happy to provide his prisoners with "luxuries" like YMCA sports equipment, band instruments, movies, and theater scripts and costumes, was invited to all the opening nights and thoroughly enjoyed himself. He felt that all the activity helped encourage the prisoners to accept their fate and forget the foolishness of escaping. He could not provide for their welfare if they broke out.

But what really helped the kriegies get through that depressing autumn were letters and packages from home delivered by the Red Cross. That and BBC reports received on forbidden radios announcing the progress of the war, which was turning in the Allies' favor.

There were a handful of escape attempts from North that fall, either by walking out the main gate in disguise or cutting through the wire at night, but none met with success. They did, however, help lull the Germans into thinking that the kriegies' enthusiasm for escaping was losing steam.

CHAPTER 12

CHRISTMAS COMES EARLY

November–December 1943

IN EARLY NOVEMBER, *KOMMANDANT* VON Lindeiner decided that North Compound needed a public address system for German Radio broadcasts and ordered that loudspeakers be set up around camp.

A few days later Red Noble was released from the cooler after another stay in solitary for one infraction or another. Carrying a blanket around his shoulders, the quick-witted Canadian was barely through the front gate when he noticed two reels of electrical wire sitting unattended between two newly planted telegraph poles.

A ladder was leaning against each pole with a German electrician on top wiring up a loudspeaker.

Figuring there was no way either of the workers could make it down their ladders in time to catch him, Noble headed straight for the two reels and without breaking stride grabbed one in each hand and ambled off to Hut 112. The workmen never saw a thing.

Noble dropped the first reel off in 112 where it was quickly stashed behind a false wall. The second reel he walked over to Hut 110 where he delivered it to Bushell's room and watched as the Big X's eyes grew big as saucers.

By nightfall, over 800 feet of high-quality, waterproof electrical cable was sitting safe and sound at the bottom of Dick's shaft. When digging resumed on Harry in January there would be no lack of wiring for electric lights.

The workmen were too afraid of being punished to report the missing reels. It was a mistake they would later regret.

Put something owned by the Germans in front of a kriegie and he would steal it. It was as natural as breathing or being hungry. One of the very few exceptions were the toolboxes loaned out on the "parole" or "word of honor" system to prisoners so they could build their theater and construct sets for plays and revues. The parole system was not to be violated and no toolbox item ever went missing.

Not so the contents of a chauffeur-driven limousine belonging to a visiting general.

Later that fall a shiny black Czech Tatra rolled into camp and parked between Huts 101 and 103 near the main gate. Built in 1938 before the Nazis seized control of Czechoslovakia, the streamlined Tatra had a third front headlight, fender skirts, and side doors that both opened toward the middle on the same hinges. But what really brought the kriegies running was the sound of its rear-mounted, V-8 engine and the aerodynamic back hood that covered it. The hood had a fin down the middle that made it look like something out of a *Flash Gordon* comic strip.

The car's owner was a jolly-looking Luftwaffe general in riding breeches and a greatcoat who was in Sagan for an official visit and tour of the camp. As he and von Lindeiner climbed out of the limo they were quickly surrounded by a swarm of automobile enthusiasts who had never seen anything like the Tatra before and pressed in for a closer look.

Knowing his prisoners were probably up to no good, the *Kommandant* ordered them away from the car but his tut-tutting guest said the men could look all they liked.

"There is no problem," he said. "My chauffeur will keep watch."

"As you wish, Herr General," said von Lindeiner, "but please make sure the windows and doors are locked."

The chauffeur was no match for the kriegies. One minute he was at the driver's side door accepting a cigarette and answering questions from German speakers. The next minute he was at the back of the car trying to get rid of several peacetime mechanics who had popped the rear hood to inspect the engine. Meanwhile, someone else had jimmied open the right front passenger door and made off with a pair of gloves, flashlight, three road maps, a tool kit, and the backseat cigarette lighter. A military handbook marked "SECRET" also disappeared before the door was closed and locked again. The break-in took less than three minutes.

The next morning an angry von Lindeiner called acting SBO Wings Day to his office. The *Kommandant* said the prisoners had disgraced the camp by burglarizing the general's car but that the general was willing to overlook the incident if the handbook was returned that afternoon.

"Make no mistake, Wing Commander," said the *Kommandant*. "This is not a request. We must have the book. You understand the situation."

"I am surprised to hear about this," said Day, who wasn't surprised at all. "Let me make some inquiries and I'll see what can be done."

The German speakers had gone through the handbook and found very little of value. Before returning it, however, Bushell had Tim Walenn's forgers make up a special boot-heel stamp and applied it to the bottom of the title page in red ink. It read: "Approved by the British Board of Censors."

December brought snow and a bitter cold east wind to Sagan, but most of the prisoners were determined to make the best of it, especially the ones who hoped to escape in the new year.

In a letter home, Bushell wrote: "It can't last much longer. This is definitely our last Christmas in the bag."

Red Cross parcels arrived with extra rations of chocolate and more than a few barracks rooms had hoarded their food for Christmas dinners and their raisins for kriegie brews.

The theater was worth its weight in holiday gold, frankincense, and myrrh. The prisoners' Christmas Revue was a roaring success, particularly the off-color skits that even von Lindeiner laughed at. And there was even a bit of Hollywood with the showing of the five-year-old Cary Grant and Katharine Hepburn screwball comedy *Bringing Up Baby.*

But the highpoint of the holiday happened outside under the stars.

After lights-out on Christmas Eve, a Yank bugler played "Silent Night" while both the British and American camps listened in absolute quiet and thought of home.

CHAPTER 13

HARRY REOPENS
FOR BUSINESS

January–February 1944

ROGER BUSHELL'S NEW YEAR'S RESOLUTION
was to catch the Germans napping.

On January 7 the "Big X" called a meeting of the escape
committee in the library room of Hut 110 and said he
wanted to reopen Harry as soon as possible. It had been
four months since he ordered it sealed following the ferrets' accidental discovery of Tom and it was time to get
the diggers back to work.

The Germans would never expect it. The accepted

escape season ended in November and didn't start up again until the ground thawed and warm weather returned in the spring. Bushell said he wanted to have Harry finished by the end of winter so they could send 200 men through the tunnel before April.

The meeting included Wings Day, Bushell's adjutant Conk Canton, chief engineer Wally Floody, Crump Ker-Ramsey (who was in charge of Harry), sand dispersal chief Hornblower Fanshawe, security chief George Harsh, his deputies George McGill and Tom Kirby-Green, and five "Little X's," or barracks bosses, who had been recently added to the committee to represent all fifteen barracks Little X's.

All agreed that Harry would be reopened on January 10 with Floody and Crump inspecting the tunnel and making any repairs necessary. Digging would resume the day after repairs were completed.

Barring a massive sand fall since being closed in September, Harry currently ran about seventy-five feet toward the *Vorlager* from its starting point under Hut 104. Floody said his surveyors estimated that the distance to the trees beyond the north fence and the road outside the compound was another 260 feet.

He added that two halfway houses, or changeover stops for the trolley line, would be needed for Harry. They would be built when the tunnel reached 100 feet and again when it pushed past 220 feet.

The unresolved problem was that old bugaboo, getting rid of the sand. With Dick's tunnel already re-filled in the rush to get Tom finished last summer and the compound sitting under a foot of snow, there seemed to be only two options. Either dump the sand under the barracks or stash it inside. Harsh and the Little X's shot down both ideas immediately, saying the ferrets would catch on in less than a week.

After an hour of getting nowhere, Bushell adjourned the meeting by telling everyone to think about where to hide the sand. Fanshawe and Crump discussed the problem as they left Hut 110 and headed south for a walk around the camp perimeter. Passing Hut 120 and coming upon the theater they stopped, turned to each other, and practically shouted "Under the theater!" at the same time.

• • •

The theater was perfect.

Its 350 seats, all made from wooden Red Cross crates, were arranged in fourteen rows that sloped gradually upward to give every member of the audience a clear view of the stage. The rows were divided into three sections by two aisles.

The incline of the floor rose over three feet from front to back and was supported underneath by wooden bracing down the middle and below the aisles. That created four huge wedges of open space under the floor to dump sand—more than enough room to handle Harry. Not only that, the kriegie-built theater rested on a foundation of solid brick so the ferrets couldn't snoop around underneath.

Everyone thought that using the theater as the dump-site was a brilliant idea, everyone except the acting troupe that ran the place.

Bushell broke the news to his fellow thespians that afternoon. They protested that if sand was found anywhere in the building the Germans might shut the theater down and with it one of the few real morale-boosting enterprises in camp. Wings Day tactfully reminded the troupers that they were prisoners of war first and actors second. Escaping was more important. End of argument.

Johnny Travis was brought in to cut a trapdoor at the rear of the theater. With a wide standing room area behind the last row he had plenty of room to hinge on the rear legs of any seat to the floor so it could be tipped backwards. Travis picked seat No. 13 for luck. Using one of his homemade saws, he then went to work on the floor beneath the chair and cut out a two-foot square that fit back into place exactly. When he was finished even Bushell couldn't tell which seat the trap was under.

With former dispersal organizer Jerry Sage now in South Compound with the rest of the Americans, Fanshawe picked veteran Brit escapers Jimmy James and Ian Cross to headman the cross-camp dump runs from Hut 104 to the theater.

Sunset during the winter ranged from 4:30 in the

afternoon in mid-January to 6 P.M. in mid-March. That meant that all trips to the theater would be sent out after dark for three to four hours each night before lock-in at ten o'clock.

The darkness and cold weather provided excellent cover for the penguins, who would no longer be asked to carry two eight-pound bags of sand in their pants and pull the pins at assigned outdoor drop points. Now they would carry two twenty-pound bags on a sling around their shoulders and inside a greatcoat.

One problem that cropped up was the telltale odor of fresh sand throughout the theater. James and Cross overcame it with a more powerful aroma. They placed smoldering tins of tobacco underneath the theater floor whenever the building was in use. Audience members who smoked pipes and cigarettes were also encouraged to light up early and often, meaning an extra thick haze of smoke would hang in the air during every play and film that winter.

· · ·

While Fanshawe and his team worked out their dispersal plans, Harry was unsealed by its "trapfuhrer" Pat Langford on January 10.

After the stove was moved and the concrete trap lifted out, Floody and Crump went down to inspect the tunnel. They found it in better condition than they expected. The air in the shaft was fresh because Crump had left the intake valve open when they closed up shop in September. Better yet, as Floody trolleyed up to the face of the tunnel he found no major sand falls and only six shoring frames that needed replacing.

The forced-air ventilation system, however, was in bad

A typical stove in one of the huts. A stove like this one sat on top of the entrance to Harry

shape and had to be overhauled. The bellows on the air pump had rotted out and most of the air pipe to the face either leaked or was clogged with sand. To replace the bellows and pipe was painstaking work that took up most of the four days needed to get the tunnel back in working order.

When that was done, the first 120 feet or so of Red Noble's stolen electric cable was hooked up to the camp's power supply and run over to Harry's trap through a space under the floor. From there it was fed down the shaft and up to the face on hooks hung from the tunnel roof. With the electricity on in camp for most of the afternoon and all night during the winter months, diggers would have to cope with fat lamps for only a few hours on the morning shift.

Digging resumed down Harry after morning *appell* on January 14. Floody and the first shift extended the tunnel ten feet that day and the revised march of the penguins to the theater went off without a hitch that night.

To help protect the penguins, Bushell increased the nighttime foot traffic in camp by getting Senior British Officer Massey to persuade the *Kommandant* to let the prisoners walk between barracks until lock-in at 10 P.M.

Within a week Harry passed 100 feet in length, which put it directly underneath the cooler. If they lay still, diggers could hear the sound of guards' jackboots on the concrete floor thirty feet above them.

The tunnel's first changeover stop was built at the 110-foot mark. The stop was called Piccadilly Circus after London's famous road junction and roundabout (the Latin word *circus* means circle). Like the changeover in Tom, Piccadilly was eight feet long and about six inches higher and wider than the rest of the tunnel. It was also the end of the line for the first run of trolley tracks and the beginning of the second run to the next changeover.

While the tunnel progressed below, up in Room 23 of Hut 104, Langford and an assistant practiced shaving seconds off the time it took them to close Harry's trap in the event of a surprise visit by the Germans. During the day the trap was shut, but at night it was wide open as the sand was hoisted up in carrying bags for the penguins to take to the theater.

Langford's two-man trap-closing drill involved seven steps:

1: Alert the crew down Harry that a snap search was under way;

2: Fit the basket grill into the shaft opening and fill the basket with used blankets to muffle the hollowness of the shaft below;

3: Lower the tiled concrete trap over the grill;

4: Slip the extension pipe off the flue leading from the chimney to the stove;

5: Using two specially fitted pieces of wood, lift the red-hot stove from alongside the trap to directly on top of it;

6: Re-attach the stove flue to the chimney;

7: Sweep away any loose sand and dust.

By the end of January, Langford had reduced the time in closing the trap to an astonishing twenty seconds. Good thing, too. A few nights later, Rubberneck and a posse of guards marched into camp and headed for the north end Hut 104.

The duty pilot at the main gate sent a runner to 104 to warn George Harsh that trouble was on the way. Harsh, who ran his security operation out of 104, chased the penguins over to Hut 109. He then ordered every remaining kriegie in the barracks to gather at the north entrance and get in the Germans' way.

Unfortunately, the goons were all elbows and rifles and quickly burst through the door and started their room-to-room search. Room 23 and Harry's trap were right near the doorway and Harsh was afraid Langford hadn't had enough time to shut the trap and replace the stove.

But he had. When Harsh reached the room the stove was standing on the trap and Langford was beside it having a cup of tea while two goons tore the room apart and found nothing.

As Rubberneck and his raiders advanced down the hall turning every room in Hut 104 upside down, Harsh asked Langford how he did it.

Langford gave the "Big S" a big smile and said, "Practice makes perfect."

While Rubberneck had no idea how far along Harry was, the head ferret was sure there was a tunnel going on the north side of camp. But his near-miss in Hut 104 wasn't the reason Bushell suspended all digging and sand carrying activity the week of February 5–11.

It was the full moon.

For seven straight cloudless nights the dazzling midwinter moonlight lit up the snow-covered compound like it was daytime. With no cover, the penguins, wrapped in their greatcoats and weighed down by two twenty-pound bags of sand, would have been easily spotted from the goon boxes. Sending them out was too dangerous.

"Bloody moon," grumbled Bushell.

The escape, when it finally went off, would not be scheduled early in the month but late. Under the complete darkness of a *new* moon.

CHAPTER 14

RUBBERNECK STRIKES

February 1944

BY FEBRUARY 12 THE FULL MOON OVER Stalag Luft III had waned enough to reopen Harry and resume sand-carrying trips to the theater.

Wally Floody dug a record twelve and half feet the first day back as the tunnel reached the 200-foot mark, but he hit a soft spot in the roof the next day and was buried under a couple hundred pounds of sand. Floody's digging partner Crump Ker-Ramsey needed Conk Canton to crawl up from the Piccadilly changeover to help pull Wally out by his legs.

Floody was quickly revived and insisted on staying below to clean up the mess. His accident was the first of several that week after seven days of inactivity.

The run of mishaps in the shaft ended on February 15 as the tunneling teams regained their momentum and Harry was pushed out to 220 feet. That put the face of the tunnel beneath the outer north fence and within 130 feet of the woods. A second changeover stop was built and called Leicester Square (pronounced "Lester") after the small park in London's West End.

For the hopeful escapers of North Compound, getting out of Stalag Luft III and making it home meant leaving Piccadilly and Leicester Square behind.

At this point an inspection by surveyors determined that Harry was one foot out of line to the right. Since no shoring that had already been installed could be removed to fix the curve, diggers brought the tunnel back in line with a gradual course correction to the left over the first five feet out of Leicester Square.

Measuring the direction of the tunnel was done with two surveyor's compasses that had been stolen from the

Germans. The length of the tunnel was calculated with a hundred-foot cord of braided string tied together from Red Cross parcels and pre-measured with a ruler. The engineers' calculations inside the tunnel were precise. Up top, however, their reckoning of the true distance from Harry's shaft to the woods past the north fence was no more than an educated guess.

There was a lot riding on the guess that it was no more than 350 feet to those trees.

With Harry two-thirds completed, Roger Bushell and the escape committee turned their attention to deciding which prisoners would participate in the 200-man breakout. Close to 600 men had been involved in the three-tunnel project in one form or another since the opening of North Compound ten and a half months ago. When the committee asked the barracks Little X's to find out how many of the 600 were interested in escaping, it got back 510 names. That meant 310 men were going to be disappointed.

Instituting a priority system, the committee determined that the 200 escapers would be chosen as follows:

The first thirty men through the tunnel would be those with the best chance of getting out of Germany and back to England. Picked by the committee, almost all of them would have to be fluent in German or other foreign languages and know the territory along their planned escape routes. They would travel in two-man teams and be provided with the best in forged papers and civilian clothes. They would also leave Sagan by train, which meant it was vital they all reach the railway station a half-mile from camp before the last trains left between 11:00 P.M. and midnight.

The next group of twenty would be drawn from the prisoners who had done the most work digging the tunnels. The third group of twenty would be drawn from all the forgers, carpenters, tin-bashers, tailors, compass-makers, and mapmakers.

The next thirty would be drawn from all the penguins, stooges, duty pilots, and runners.

A second-chance draw for eighty names would come

from the 410 candidates not chosen so far, and the last twenty slots would go to deserving men who had not yet drawn a place.

While the first thirty men in line were expected to make the Sagan station in plenty of time to board their trains, the other 170 escapers were on their own. If they could catch a train, fine, but the majority would have to get away on foot, or "hard-arse it" in British slang.

The draw took place on February 20. The teams of Bushell and Bob Tuck, and Wally Valenta and Johnny Marshall would be the first out. One change in the order of escape resulted from a suggestion by Crump that three out of every twenty escapers in line be experienced tunnelers. That way, each section of the trolley line would have a hauler to pull through twenty men before heading out himself. Also, if anything went wrong an old hand would be close by to solve the problem and keep the line moving.

Meanwhile, the attempt to divert attention from Hut 104 failed. One of the ferrets found a small trail of sand in the snow near the fire pool between huts 104 and 110. Rubberneck responded by surrounding 104 with armed guards and searching the barracks for three hours.

Nothing was found, but Walter, a German corporal who helped Pieber count heads during *appells* and had been cultivated as a contact by Valenta, told Wally that Rubberneck was convinced a tunnel was being dug. He also said Hut 110 would be searched next.

Word was passed to Bushell, who made sure that any escape-related equipment in 110 was moved to other barracks. The hut's most important inventory, the forged documents worked on every day in the library by Tim Walenn's Dean & Dawson crew, was already being taken to Hut 122 every afternoon and safely hidden at the bottom of Dick's shaft.

By late February, Valenta got a tip from Walter that Rubberneck was scheduled to go on leave for two weeks starting March 1.

What a break. A gleeful Floody told the escape committee that with less than a hundred feet to go he could speed up work in Harry and have the tunnel finished, exit shaft and all, by the time Rubberneck returned. Then all they had to do was seal it up and wait for a new moon and decent weather to break out.

Bushell and Harsh were more apprehensive. They figured Rubberneck would take another crack at them before his vacation.

Bushell guessed it would be one or two snap roll calls in the middle of the day to catch one of the eight-man digging teams down in the tunnel. To foil any surprise head counts, he had Pat Langford come up with an emergency plan to evacuate Harry in a hurry and instructed all the Little X's to tell their barracks to make their way as slowly as possible to the *appell* ground.

Harsh thought Rubberneck had something more insidious up his sleeve, but he had no idea what.

They were both right.

At lunchtime two days later, Rubberneck led twenty guards into camp to chase the prisoners out of their huts for a snap roll call. Harsh was outside Hut 104 and saw them come through the main gate. He relayed word to

Langford in Room 23 and Pat set the new evacuation drill in motion by getting the stove moved and the trap opened in less than fifteen seconds. They then hollered down the hole: "Ferrets! Get Out!".

Flashlights signaled the alert from the bottom of the shaft up to the haulers at the Piccadilly and Leicester Square changeovers and on to the face of the tunnel. The diggers dropped what they were doing and trolleyed back as fast as they could.

Luckily, the Germans botched any chance they might have had to catch the tunnelers red-handed when the guards were ordered to fall in and count off before being dismissed to clear out the barracks. That bow to military procedure cost them over a minute. It also took them so long to chase the foot-dragging kriegies out of huts 101 and 103 that by the time they reached 104 the tunnelers were long gone and Harry was locked up tight.

But 1944 was a leap year and on February 29, the day before the start of his two-week leave, Rubberneck finally jumped on Bushell's escape plans with both feet.

Interrupting the regular morning roll call, the hated

head ferret appeared on the *appell* ground with Broili and a posse of thirty armed guards. Clipboard in hand, Broili stepped forward and announced that the nineteen officers whose names he was about to read off were being transferred to Belaria, a Luftwaffe prison compound five miles away.

Some of the names belonged to diggers and penguins who had been working on Harry, but others had no connection to the tunnel at all. Two of the names—Bob Tuck, who roomed with Bushell, and Jim Tyrie, one of Valenta's best contact men—caused some concern. But it was the last three names called that stunned everyone involved with the escape: Floody, Fanshawe, and Harsh. Bushell's top three lieutenants.

The nineteen were searched, marched to the main gate without being allowed to gather their things, then put on a transport truck and sent directly to Belaria. Floody, Fanshawe, and Harsh cursed their bad luck. Later they would feel differently.

And how did Bushell escape the purge?

The theater again. He had the lead role of Professor

Higgins in the upcoming camp production of *Pygmalion*. When Rubberneck and the ferrets drew up their hit list of likely escape ringleaders, they must have figured that anyone rehearsing for a play scheduled to debut at the end of March wouldn't be trying to leave camp before then.

CHAPTER 15

HARRY IS READY TO GO

March 1–18, 1944

THE X-ORGANIZATION'S PLAN TO BREAK 200 men out of North Compound had become such a well-oiled machine that losing its three key division chiefs didn't matter. If anything, their forced removal from camp was further motivation for the remaining escapers to succeed.

Wally Floody and George Harsh were immediately replaced by their very capable number twos, Crump Ker-Ramsey as tunnel boss and George McGill as Big S, the head of security. Hornblower Fanshawe's sand dispersal operation was running so smoothly that he didn't need to be replaced at all.

If there was a guy who couldn't be replaced, it was Rubberneck. No other ferret or guard in camp treated the prisoners with such contempt and was so loathed in return. Rubberneck suspected every kriegie of trying to dig his way out of Stalag Luft III and every barracks of hiding a tunnel. With him on leave for two weeks there was a gaping hole in compound security. The Germans had no backup ferrets obsessed with finding escape tunnels.

Crump told Bushell that the diggers were ready to mount an all-out effort to finish Harry and construct an exit shaft before Rubberneck returned on March 15.

Shifting into high gear, the underground crews pushed twelve feet closer to the woods on March 3 and advanced a record fourteen feet a day later. By March 11 the tunnel was completed with the building of an eight-foot-long staging area leading up to the spot where the exit shaft would be.

Harry now stretched 348 feet, a foot and a half longer

than the soccer field at the Olympic Stadium in Berlin. It was also thirteen feet longer than the distance escape committee surveyors figured was needed to reach the woods. All the shoring was in place, air-lines buried, electrical cable hung, trolley tracks laid, and sand sent back down the tunnel for dispersal. It was a thing of beauty.

There were now just three days left before Rubberneck returned and it would take all of that time to manage the difficult and dangerous job of excavating the exit shaft.

Given the way the ground fell away from the main road outside the north fence, the surveyors figured the exit shaft would be no more than twenty-five feet in length. Johnny Travis and his carpenters had already prepared the bedboards needed for the solid box framing of the two-foot-square shaft. A twenty-four-foot ladder had also been built and divided into three-foot sections that could be reassembled as the shaft gained height.

The problem with digging vertically was gravity.

There was no place for the falling clumps of sand to go but right in the lead digger's face. Travis made a board shield so Crump could dig upwards on one side of the shaft and then the other while keeping the sand from falling on him. The shield worked well but holding it up with one hand and digging with the other for a prolonged length of time was murder on the arms.

As the shaft rose from the tunnel floor it was framed and boarded on all four sides every three feet. The work was slow at first but the diggers picked up momentum as they went along and reached the nineteen-foot mark just before *appell* on the afternoon of March 14. Crump and Johnny Marshall thought they still had six or seven feet to go when they came upon some pine tree roots and realized they were actually less than two feet from daylight. They could hardly contain their excitement as they trolleyed back to attend roll call and tell Bushell the news.

After *appell*, Crump sent Johnny Bull and Red Noble down for the late shift with instructions to find out exactly how close the exit shaft was to the surface. Fellow digger Danny Krol, who had been a fencing champion in Poland before the war, gave Bull his YMCA-issued foil to do the job. The light, three-foot sword had a thin, flexible blade with a protective button affixed to the point. Krol had snipped off the button to help it slide through the sand and earth above.

Bull had barely nudged the blade into the ground over his head when he felt it poke though the dirt and snow and into the cold night air. He marked the blade on his end and pulled the sword back through the ground. There was no need to measure it. Only six inches of topsoil separated Harry from the outside world.

Scrambling down the ladder to tell Red, Johnny had just reached the last rung when they heard the sound of rolling thunder overhead.

"What the hell was that?" said Red.

Before Johnny could answer, another ear-splitting rumble passed over them.

"Trucks," he said. "We must be too close to the road."

Climbing back up the ladder, Bull put a roof on the

shaft, securing it with a removable box frame. He also made sure to pack a foot of sand between the top of the frame and the patch of ground yet to be dug out. The bracing was necessary to make sure the ground could hold the weight of any perimeter guards who might step directly on it.

As Bull and Noble headed back up the tunnel they collected every piece of unused or no longer useful material they could find. When the last of the extra bedposts, bed boards, air pipe milk tins, electrical cord, tools, and trolley sand boxes were hauled out of the entry shaft, Pat Langford closed and sealed Harry for the last time before the night of the escape. The spare parts were either burned the next day or stored down Dick.

Harry was officially completed sixty-four days after it was reopened on January 10.

Bull and Noble told Bushell and Crump about the rumbling trucks. Bushell thought the sound must have been amplified by the sand and being at the bottom of a nineteen-foot shaft. Nevertheless, he ordered the surveyors to double check their calculations. The surveyors ran their numbers again and said they were confident the exit shaft was safely inside the woods.

Rubberneck was back on duty March 15 and waited only until after lunch to pull a snap search of Hut 104.

A squad of ferrets and guards came running through the main gate and made straight for 104. They had flushed the last kriegies out of the barracks just as Rubberneck made his dramatic entrance through the front door. The hut had been cleared of all escape-related equipment the night before and Langford had been a fanatic about disguising the trap in Room 23, but the four-hour search had everyone on edge. Only when the Germans gave up and walked out did breathing return to normal.

At the escape committee meeting that night, it was agreed that the breakout had to be soon. Before the end of the month.

The next new moon would provide complete darkness from Thursday night March 23 through Saturday night

March 25. Bushell eliminated Saturday night because so few trains ran on Sunday. After an hour's discussion on the best night to go, Roger picked Friday the 24th as the tentative date. He would make the final decision by 11:00 in the morning of that day.

Kommandant von Lindeiner made a point of remembering the birthdays of all the Allied senior officers. So, on March 18 he walked a bottle of champagne over to Hut 101 and presented it to Squadron Leader Bill Jennens with his compliments.

Jennens, who was fluent in German, thanked the *Kommandant* for his thoughtfulness and invited him to stay for a drink or two as he popped the cork and filled the tin cups eagerly held out by his seven roommates.

Rising to leave a half-hour later, von Lindeiner buttoned up his greatcoat, gestured to the falling snow outside, and said that after a fairly mild January and February, this was the coldest March in Germany in thirty years. He got no arguments from his hosts, who were all huddled in blankets around the room's coal-burning stove.

After shaking hands all around and accepting a final toast of thanks, the *Kommandant* paused at the door and said: "I almost forgot to ask, Squadron Leader. How is the tunneling coming?"

"What!" replied Jennens, caught off guard but recovering nicely. "In this weather?"

Everyone laughed, including von Lindeiner who, like Rubberneck, knew something was in the works. He also knew something the escapers didn't know and it worried him.

The German High Command had issued an order stating that effective immediately any recaptured prisoner of war holding an officer's rank was to be handed over to the Gestapo rather than returned to the appropriate military authority. It also said that POW officers should not be told of this order.

This was contrary to the Geneva Convention that protected all POWs as long as they didn't break any laws or attack any citizens.

Bushell, however, knew from firsthand experience that the Gestapo played by its own rules. As a two-time escaper he also knew that they would be gunning for him if he ever got out again, but he wasn't worried. "Next time," he told Jennens, "they won't catch me."

A follow-up order from Gestapo headquarters in Berlin said that all recaptured prisoner of war officers, other than British and Americans, were to be taken in chains to Mauthausen Concentration Camp in Austria and executed. Nothing was said about what would happen to the Brits and Yanks.

After receiving these orders, von Lindeiner called a meeting of the senior officers, doctors, and chaplains from all the four compounds of Stalag Luft III. He wasn't allowed to read them the Gestapo memo but he tried to warn them.

"Please, gentlemen," he said, "the war may be over in a year or two. It is not worth taking unnecessary risks now."

With Harry ready to go, nobody in North Compound was listening.

CHAPTER 16

TONIGHT'S THE NIGHT

March 20–24, 1944

THE GREAT ESCAPE WAS GOING TO HAPPEN the night of March 24. When Roger Bushell made that decision on March 15, he said the date was conditional on the weather, but anyone who knew Roger knew that his mind was made up. Barring a blizzard or some other unforeseen calamity, the biggest jailbreak of the war could wait no longer.

Rubberneck had his tunnel-finding sights on Hut 104 and the odds were that he'd find Harry—by accident, probably, like his ferrets discovered Tom—but he'd find it eventually. The trapdoor in Room 23 had developed a wobble after nine months under a red-hot stove and keeper Pat Langford couldn't guarantee it would hold out another month. And a winter escape would still surprise the hell out of the Germans. They might know the kriegies had a tunnel in progress, but they had no idea it was finished and ready to pop.

When the "Go" date was set, the clock started ticking for all the X-Organization's support industries. The departments responsible for everything from forging travel papers to cooking up concentrated energy bars for the road to plotting the traffic flow to Hut 104 the night of the escape so that the guards wouldn't get suspicious, had nine days to meet their deadlines.

Tim Walenn's forgery factory, nicknamed the Dean & Dawson Travel Agency, had the most work still to do. The forgers not only had to finish turning out more than 400 fake passes, identity cards, and other documents, they also had to make sure each of the documents conformed with the cover story concocted for each escaper.

After protecting Harry, guarding those forged

documents was the most important security job in camp. They were kept in four waterproof metal cans and stored down Dick below the Hut 122 washroom. Stooges babysitting the forgers' workplace in the library of Hut 110 picked up and brought back the cans twice a day, morning and afternoon. Walenn insisted the cans be returned to the tunnel during lunchtime.

The most elaborate cover stories belonged to the first thirty men out of the tunnel. These fifteen two-man teams were considered the best bets to make it all the way back to England by virtue of their language skills and knowledge of the countries they would be traveling through. They would also need as many as six documents to back up their stories.

Bushell, for instance, was headed west to Paris with Free French pilot Bernard Scheidhauer, who replaced Bob Tuck as Bushell's running mate after Tuck was transferred to another POW camp in the surprise purge of February 29. Bushell and Scheidhauer were posing as French businessmen and not only needed passes and ID cards, but also bogus letters of credit and business correspondence as well.

Wings Day, on the other hand, was impersonating an Irish traitor named "Colonel Brown," who was captured by the Germans in 1940 and had since become an avowed Nazi. He would be traveling north to Berlin and then Stettin escorted by a Luftwaffe corporal played by Peter Tobolski, a stocky blond Polish pilot fluent in German. The forgers had fun making up "official" propaganda ministry documents proclaiming Col. Brown's allegiance to the Third Reich and Tobolski had managed to steal a genuine Luftwaffe airman's pay book and travel warrant.

Tob also had a Luftwaffe uniform made for him by Tommy Guest and his tailoring shop that was indistinguishable from the real thing. By March 24, Guest's mainly Polish and Czech tailors would have hand-sewn nearly fifty civilian suits out of RAF uniforms, blankets, and any other material they could find that would have been the envy of most clothiers in London, let alone Berlin.

The suits went to train travelers who needed to look

like the lawyers, accountants, and businessmen they claimed to be. The cross-country travelers or hard-arsers, who had to get away on foot, staying off main roads and tramping through the snow, were all dressed as foreign workers.

With tips from the tailors, all of these kriegies did their own altering. They shaved the serge fuzz off RAF uniforms with a razor blade, modified their stiff-collared tunics to look more rustic, made cloth caps from blankets, and dyed their jackets and trousers with beet-root juice and boot polish solution. Another trick they learned was waterproofing their boots with margarine. Most were headed south to Czechoslovakia which was sixty miles away.

The hard-arsers would all need compasses and maps. The last of 200 compasses had rolled off Al Hake's production line in Hut 103 in January and were all stored down Dick and ready to go. Des Plunkett's mapmaking operation was nearly completed. His ingenious gelatin-powered mimeograph copying system would produce more than 3,000 local, national, and regional maps by the 24th.

Ace scrounger Axel Zillessen had a tamed ferret who helped him put together a detailed map of all the paths through the woods to the Sagan railway station. He also gave Zillessen an up-to-date timetable of all the trains leaving Sagan. Those tables were reproduced on a small printing press made by Johnny Travis and his carpentry shop. Travis's crew also cut up hundreds of food tins and soldered them into 200 leakproof hip flasks for carrying water.

Eric Lubbock, a Royal Navy dietician and nutritional expert, came up with a recipe for a high-energy fudge bar to keep hard-arsers on the go. The concentrated escape food consisted of powdered milk, sugar, cocoa, vitamin pills, oatmeal, raisins, crushed biscuits, glucose, and margarine. In the four days leading up the breakout, a dozen cooks in Hut 112 made 180 pounds of the stuff and Johnny Travis's tin-bashers packed it into 720 four-ounce cocoa tins. Each tin had enough calories for two days on the run. Hard-arsers were given four tins each and train travelers got two.

Bushell's dream of busting 200 POWs out in one night was mathematically unrealistic and he knew it. The escape window was only eight and a half hours, from 9 P.M. to sunrise the next morning at 5:30. That's 510 minutes. Under ideal conditions with nothing going wrong, the average tunnel break might get one man out every two minutes.

But this was no average tunnel break. It was the largest one ever attempted. Not only that, it involved mostly inexperienced escapers bundled in winter clothes making their way through a cramped, 348-foot tunnel that was sensitive to cave-ins.

If they managed to get one man out every four minutes (for a total of 127) they would be very lucky. One man every five minutes (for a total of 102) was more likely. Still, Bushell wanted 200 men on deck and ready to go in case, by some miracle, everything went right.

When Bushell's group of train travelers was subjected

to the mock interrogations, the Big X, who had been caught in two previous escape attempts, pointed out that the Gestapo had a favorite trick to catch prisoners posing as Germans or foreigners who spoke German.

"The trick," said Bushell, "is that when they end their questioning and hand you back your papers they say 'Good luck' in English. The most natural thing in the world is to answer them in English, but, gentlemen, a 'Thank you' will get you arrested. Be alert and don't fall for it."

All two-man teams with trains to catch were briefed on which paths to take through the woods to Sagan station a half-mile away. Once out of the tunnel, they were on their own.

The hard-arsers, however, needed their marshals to lead them through the woods to the west of Stalag Luft III and past some nearby camps and military outposts to a little dirt road headed south to Czechoslovakia. Each marshal would climb out of the exit hole, wait in the woods for all ten of his men to join him, then set off.

•   •   •

On March 22, Crump and Johnny Marshall began two days of lectures to make sure all escapers knew how to navigate the tunnel.

The talks boiled down to seven dos and don'ts: 1.) Lie completely flat on the trolleys; 2.) Keep your head down and your elbows in; 3.) Hold your suitcases or carrying bags out in front of you length-wise; 4.) Let the haulers pull you along and enjoy the ride; 5.) Don't tip the trolley; 6.) If you *do* tip the trolley and it comes off the rails, crawl forward to the next changeover station and pull the rope attached to the trolley along with you; and 7.) No matter what happens, don't panic. Squirming around might dislodge the framing and cause a sand fall.

Crump then inspected each escaper's getaway outfit and the suitcase or bag they expected to take with them. He didn't hesitate to disqualify anything that looked bulky enough to tip over a trolley and clog the tunnel. His main concern was to keep the trolleys moving and get as many men out as possible.

The hard-arsers were not expected to make it out of occupied territory and back to England. Their job was to stay on the loose for as long as possible and make as many German troops as possible search for them. With that in mind, Wing Commander John Ellis, an outdoor survival expert, gave them some tips on roughing it cross-country in the dead of winter.

It snowed the night of March 23 and the *Pygmalion* dress rehearsal went well. Bushell's performance in the lead role of Henry Higgins was terrific and gave no hint of the drama to come 24 hours later.

At 11:30 the next morning, the escape committee met in Bushell's room in Hut 110. The meeting lasted just ten minutes. The only presentation made was by Len Hall, late of the RAF Meteorological Branch, who delivered the weather report for that night. As far as he could tell, it would be cloudy and very cold, but it wasn't going to snow.

Bushell looked around the room and said, "Anyone have a problem with going tonight?"

Nobody did.

"Right. Then tonight's the night."

The room, antsy at the start of the meeting, was now electric. Bushell closed his final meeting as Big X by saying, "I imagine you've all got things to do, so let's get cracking."

Fifteen minutes after the meeting broke up, the entire compound seemed to know the escape was on. Jimmy James, who was No. 39 on the escape list, would later refer to the mood that swept over the camp as "a fever of excitement." Security chief George McGill feared that the Germans could feel it too, but they couldn't. Not yet.

Tim Walenn walked down the hall of Hut 110 to the library where his fellow Dean & Dawson travel agents were waiting at desks piled high with counterfeit identity cards, police permits, and other documents needed by the escapers. Tim gave his forgers a thumbs-up and they immediately began "authenticating" all 400 of the travel papers with imitation date stamps cut from rubber boot heels by Al Hake.

Any documents that required the signatures of government officials or chiefs of police were handled by Alex

Cassie and Gordon Brettell. They either penned spot-on copies of real signatures obtained by contacts or scribbled fake names that looked gaudy enough to be real. By waiting until the last possible moment, the escapers would be able to get maximum use out of any limited-time permits.

Crump Ker-Ramsey, Conk Canton, and Pat Langford hustled back to Hut 104 where Pat reopened Harry, and Crump and Conk climbed down to prepare the tunnel for a busy night.

Making Harry escape-ready meant tripling the number of lightbulbs in the tunnel. The idea was that the additional light would calm the nerves of those prone to claustrophobia.

Once that was done, Crump and Conk had to modify the three trolleys for heavy-duty use. They also replaced the ropes needed to haul the trolleys to and from each changeover area. The rope—over 400 feet of one-inch-thick manilla cord from the Philippines—was originally intended for the camp's boxing ring and had arrived from the YMCA only a week before.

The forgers finished up by mid-afternoon, handing the travel documents off to the fifteen Little X's who distributed them to each of the escapers in their respective huts. Crump and Conk, however, were far from done when they came up for afternoon *appell* at five o'clock.

Still on their to-do list was muffling the sound of trolley traffic out of the entry and exit shafts. To do that they would nail cloth strips to the first fifty feet and last fifty feet of the trolley tracks. They also had to hang two blackout blankets below the exit shaft to absorb noise and block any light from getting out.

Finally, blankets would need to be spread over the Piccadilly and Leicester Square changeover areas to keep escapers' clothes from getting too dirty as they crawled from trolley to trolley.

Shortly before afternoon *appells* in the British and American compounds, word reached Bub Clark on the American side of the fence that Bushell wanted to talk to him. Making sure there were no Germans around to eavesdrop, Roger called over to Bub with the expected news.

"We go tonight," he said. "Please don't do anything to screw it up."

"Wouldn't dream of it," said Clark, meaning the Yanks had nothing planned. "Good luck, Roger. Take care of yourself."

"Thanks," said Bushell. "See you in London."

At around six o'clock little farewell suppers were taking place in rooms all over camp as escapers had a last hot meal before packing up and making their way to Hut 104.

Outside the night was colder than Hitler's heart, with a biting breeze that led one of Jimmy James's roommates to say, "I wouldn't put a dog out on a night like this."

In Hut 119 out by the theater, hard-arsers Red Noble and Shag Rees dressed as warmly as they could—long-johns, wool pants, heavy socks, boots, shirt, long-sleeved vest, heavy pullover, greatcoat, scarf, gloves, and cloth cap with earflaps. They stuffed their pockets with tins of road fudge, a flask of water, maps, a compass, travel papers, matches, and an extra pair of socks. Luckily, after a year and half as POWs they were so thin that even with all that on they'd still be able to fit in the tunnel.

As with every other phase of the operation the procession of escapers to Hut 104 was designed to keep the Germans in the dark by not attracting attention.

The schedule called for one escaper to enter Hut 104 every 30 seconds from seven o'clock to nine. Central to the success of the scheme was luring Rudi the ferret, the regular Friday night watchman, to the other side of camp. On this brutally cold night, Rudi was by a warm stove in Hut 112 drinking real coffee and eating a bar of chocolate with Billy Griffith and his roommates.

Even with Rudi at a safe distance, there were stooges at every window of Hut 104 on the lookout for Germans. Then a little after eight o'clock the unthinkable happened. With barracks rooms jammed and the central hallway floor filling up with chit-chatting kriegies dressed as businessmen and factory workers, the south door swung open and in walked a small but powerfully built Luftwaffe corporal.

The hallway went suddenly still. Torrens, at the opposite end of the corridor, looked up, saw the uniform, and turned white. How the hell did *he* get in here? The German headed straight for him, his heavy boots clomping on the wood floor. Torrens pulled himself together and moved forward, thinking of some way—*any way!*—to get this kraut out of the building before everything was lost. They met in the middle of the hall and the German spoke first.

"Hi, David. Have you seen Wings?"

It was Peter Tobolski, the Polish pilot who was traveling north with Wings Day, dressed as a German guard. Unnerved by the authentic-looking Luftwaffe outfit prepared by Tommy Guest's tailoring shop, nobody had bothered to look at Tobolski's face.

"Bloody hell, Tob," said a relieved Torrens. "You just gave us all a heart attack."

At 8:30 P.M., a half hour before the first man was due to climb out of the exit shaft, SBO Massey came by to wish Bushell and his 199 fellow escapers good luck and Godspeed.

By 8:45 Conk emerged from the open trap to say the tunnel was finally ready. Crump remained below to direct traffic and the big Frenchman Jean Staubo was working the air pump.

Now it began. Over the next 45 minutes the first fifteen men in line descended the ladder into Harry and were deployed in stages throughout the tunnel. Johnny Bull, who would open the exit at the other end, was the first one down and took the new trolley ropes from Crump. They shook hands, Bull lowered himself onto the trolley, and off he went paddling his way up to Piccadilly.

Johnny Marshall was next. He waited for Bull to reach the changeover and give two tugs on the rope. Marshall then pulled the trolley back to the entry shaft, got on, and gave the rope two tugs. That was Bull's signal to haul Marshall up to Piccadilly.

Marshall then repeated the procedure with Bushell, the third man on line. This procedure of each man pulling up the man behind him continued until the first seven men were all cheek by jowl at the exit shaft changeover.

Bull crawled to the ladder and went up to dismantle the temporary wooden roof at the top of the shaft and dig through the remaining nine inches to the surface. Everybody else waited for him to break through, except Dowse, whose job it was to haul up the next twenty escapers before he was replaced and free to go.

Back down the line, haulers with the same twenty-man quotas were also in place at Leicester Square and Piccadilly. And the trolleys at Leicester Square, Piccadilly, and the bottom of the entry shaft all had a man lying on them and another man on deck.

It was 9:30, only a half hour behind schedule. Everyone was in place and ready to go. After a year of meticulous planning and resourceful execution, the escape committee had thought of everything. Or had it?

Bull couldn't open the exit. The temporary roof was frozen solid.

Working in the dark was bad enough, but Bull was also without his favorite metal trowel. Crump had substituted a new wooden one that was supposed to make less noise breaking through the surface. Unfortunately, it was worthless at digging between frozen boards and prying them apart.

A job that should have been handled in ten minutes was taking forever. At ten o'clock, Bushell sent Marshall up the ladder to help Bull get a move on. Bull, breathing heavily and soaked with sweat, handed the trowel to Marshall saying, "You have a go, I'm done in."

Marshall stripped down to his long-johns to keep his tweed traveling suit from getting dirty, and went to work digging away at one corner of the stubborn roof. He got a toehold between two boards after ten minutes and, five minutes later, had one loosened enough to snap it in half with the trowel. The rest of the roof was then easy to pull apart.

Trading places with a revived Johnny Bull, Marshall got back into his suit as Bull dug through the last wedge of earth separating them from freedom. A blast of cool air hit him in the face and quickly ran the length of the tunnel. Crump felt it 348 feet away and called softly up to controller Jimmy Davison at the top of the shaft, "They've broken through."

. . .

The nighttime stars never looked as beautiful to Johnny Bull. He was so happy to see them twinkling above that it didn't occur to him his view was an unobstructed one.

He inched up the last two rungs of the ladder and slowly poked his head out of the hole. Now it struck him. Where were the trees? Straight ahead was the perimeter fence with the *Vorlager* beyond it, but the goonbox off to the left was only about forty-five feet away.

Turning to look over his shoulder Bull felt his heart sink. Harry was short of the woods. Instead of being fifteen feet inside the tree line, the exit hole was fifteen feet away from it. In the open. Exposed.

What were they going to do now?

CHAPTER 17

THE ESCAPE

March 24–25, 1944

"ROGER, WE HAVE A PROBLEM." JOHNNY BULL
had come back down the ladder and ducked under the
blackout blankets to deliver the grim news to Bushell and
Johnny Marshall.

Short? Marshall couldn't believe it and went up to look
for himself. He returned a minute or two later muttering
uncomplimentary things about the escape committee's
surveyors.

Bushell asked both men if they could be seen from the
goonbox.

"Doubt it," said Marshall. "The goons are too busy looking into camp so their backs are turned."

"But the perimeter guards will be trouble," said Bull. "They'll be walking right past the hole."

Working the problem out in his head, Bushell said they had two options. They could postpone the escape or go ahead with it, provided they came up with a workable plan for getting 200 men out of the exit hole and into the woods without being seen.

Postponing would allow them to extend the tunnel an additional twenty-five feet to the woods. But it would also mean waiting four weeks for the next new moon and hoping that Rubberneck didn't find Harry before then.

And then there were the documents. "All the papers are date-stamped," Bushell said. "They won't be any good a month from now. And it'll take longer than that for the forgers to make replacements. No, we've got to go tonight."

That left them with drawing up a Plan B for leaving the now exposed exit hole. Plan A had called for a controller to lie on his stomach at the exit point in the woods and tap the head of each man at the top of the ladder when it was safe to climb out. That man would then leave the hole and follow a rope line twenty yards further into the woods to a marshaling area.

Bull had an idea. "You remember those duck blinds the ferrets used to spy on us from the woods?" he asked. "Well, one of them is about ten feet from the hole. We could tie a rope to the ladder, run it over to the ferret fence, and put the controller in there. When the coast is clear, he gives the rope two tugs and the next bloke crawls out."

It was a brilliant solution and Bushell agreed to it immediately. He then pulled a pencil from his coat and printed the following instructions on the wall of the exit chamber:

1. PAUSE AT TOP OF SHAFT.
2. HOLD SIGNAL ROPE TIED TO TOP RUNG.
3. ON RECEIVING TWO TUGS, CRAWL OUT.
4. FOLLOW ROPE TO SHELTER.

When he was done, he told Sydney Dowse, who was the hauler at the exit changeover, to make sure everyone was aware of the new procedure.

Bull grabbed the coiled rope that Crump Ker-Ramsey had stashed at the foot of the ladder earlier in the day and went up to get ready. He would be the first controller behind the ferret fence. Marshall followed him, taking the rope another fifteen yards into the woods where escapers would gather in prearranged groups before setting off for the train station or the countryside.

After that, in intervals of two to three minutes, depending on the whereabouts of the patrolling perimeter guards, Wally Valenta, Bushell, Bernard Scheidhauer, and Rupert Stevens each received their two tugs. One by one they crawled out of the hole, slithered through the snow to the ferret fence, and continued to follow the rope into the woods.

The escape train was finally moving.

10:30 P.M.

With a jerk and a whoosh, the trolley at the bottom of the entry shaft zoomed off to Piccadilly Circus with an escaper and his suitcase on board. All three trolleys were now being hauled to the next changeover area up the line. Watching cart and cargo recede into the distance gave Crump a rush of excitement, but the breakout had fallen an hour and a half behind schedule.

Since there was no communications link with the front of the tunnel, the keyed-up escapers down the line had no idea what the holdup was about. The rolling trolleys and Crump's cheery "We're off!" sent up the shaft in a loud whisper to controller Jimmy Davison came as a huge relief.

11:45 P.M.

The line of escapers down the entry shaft, through the tunnel, and out the other end was proceeding at a decent clip of one every four minutes. Then came the rumble of RAF bombers headed for a night raid on Berlin.

Wings Day, who was No. 20 on the escape list, had just swung his legs over the edge of the entry shaft when the air raid sirens sounded and lights went out. The *Kommandamnt* always cut the electricity on the approach of night bombers. Wings cursed his luck as he descended the ladder. The RAF hadn't bombed Berlin in two weeks, why tonight of all nights?

The tunnel was pitch black and suddenly a terrifying place to be if you were the least bit claustrophobic. The trolleys had stopped and the haulers at Piccadilly and Leicester Square had abandoned their posts in the confusion and headed for the exit.

Panic was in the stuffy underground air, but Wings and Crump kept their heads. Crump grabbed ten fat lamps he had stored in the shaft and placed them at the front of the trolley. He lit two of them and gave Wings a box of matches. Wings put his modest suitcase farther back on the trolley, laid down on top of it, and pulled himself up to Piccadilly. He hung the first fat lamp halfway down the track and the second at the changeover. After pulling another hauler up to relieve him, he repeated the process from Piccadilly to Leicester Square.

The dependable Dowse was still on duty at the exit changeover, so he hauled Wings to the end of the line.

"What kept you?" joked Dowse, glad to see his radiant replacement appear out of the blackness.

"Thanks for sticking around," said Wings. "Now get out of here."

The train was moving again, but thirty-five more minutes had been lost. Still, without the 45-year-old Day doing the job of two men half his age, the delay would have been far worse.

1:30 A.M.

Crump's biggest worry was that an escaper or his luggage would bump into one of the tunnel's box frames and cause a sand fall. If that happened, somebody, either Crump or one of the haulers, would have to crawl up to the scene of the accident, pull out the buried victim, and repair the collapsed roofing.

The first sand fall of the night occurred while the electricity was still off. Tom Kirby-Green shifted his weight forward while being hauled from Piccadilly to Leicester Square and the back wheels of his trolley came off the track. Bundled up in a great coat, Kirby-Green pushed himself off the back of the cart to fix the wheels and his right shoulder bumped into the edge of a frame. He was buried in sand from his head to his knees in two seconds.

Hank Birkland, the big Canadian and veteran tunneler who was hauling Kirby-Green to Leicester Square, felt the line tighten and the trolley stop. Smelling trouble, he crawled back to the cave-in, pulled Kirby-Green free, and flattened himself out so Tom could crawl over him and move up the tunnel.

The nearest fat lamp had been snuffed out in the collapse, so Birkland had to repair the roof in total darkness. Lying on his back and feeling around with his hands, he refit the framing and roof boards and packed as much sand above them as he could. He did this knowing that another collapse could happen at any second. It took an hour and left Hank drenched in sweat but he got the job done and returned to Leicester Square crawling backward.

A minute later the all-clear sirens wailed outside and the lights came back on.

While the blackout had complicated the escapers' progress through the tunnel, it had actually helped them once they popped out of the exit hole. Without perimeter lighting and searchlights, the goons in the towers and on the ground outside the fence were on the alert for wire jobs. No opportunistic prisoner with a pair of wire cutters and a lot of nerve was going to catch them napping.

2:55 A.M.

With only three hours until daybreak, fewer than fifty men had made it out of the tunnel and into the woods. The train travelers, or suitcase brigade, were all gone by 2:30, although the air raid blackout had created a real mess at Sagan station. Bushell and a few others were able to catch a train west to Breslau before the sirens went off, but the rest were left to find seats on later trains.

The first of the hard-arsers, or blanket brigade, started entering the tunnel at 2:15. By then Crump had taken over as traffic controller at the top of the entry shaft and was reading the Riot Act to practically every man who stepped up to pass inspection. Yes, the hard-arsers were going to have to rough it on foot in freezing weather, but there was a limit to what they could wear and carry and still fit in the tunnel.

Everybody had two blankets (for sleeping in), but most of the bedding was either rolled up too loosely or draped too carelessly around escapers' shoulders. The blankets were a safety hazard and Crump insisted that they be folded once and rolled tightly with string or be left behind.

But blankets continued to cause delays and when a trolley rope broke between Piccadilly and Leicester Square at 3:30, the rate of escape had slowed to one man every twelve minutes. Crump realized that there was now no chance of getting more than a hundred men out before daybreak. He also knew he'd have to do something drastic to have a shot at even that many.

So he banned blankets altogether, a bone-chilling proposition that the hard-arsers took remarkably well. He than advised Dave Torrens to tell Numbers 101 through 200 on the escape list that tonight was not their night. Sorry chaps. Eat your rations and get some sleep. Many who had their long-anticipated travel plans cancelled were disappointed. Others were depressed. And a few were relieved. None would realize until later how lucky they were.

4:50 A.M.

In Hut 104, Crump and Torrens looked out the window of Room 23 and then down at their watches. The night sky was starting to brighten. With sunrise less than an hour away, they agreed to stop sending men down Harry at five o'clock. The last escaper would be No. 87.

Some 360 feet away at the ferret fence near the exit, escaper No. 76, former Olympic shot-putter and RAF air-gunner Lawrence Reavell-Carter, crawled past Langlois to the edge of the woods. He would wait there for the next group of ten hard-arsers before heading around the west side of camp and then heading south.

Canadian Keith Ogilvie was out of the hole next and snaked his way along the rope line to join Reavell-Carter. New Zealanders Mick Shand and Len Trent were in the process of doing the same when Langlois suddenly gave the rope an urgent yank in two directions. STOP! Shand had just passed the ferret fence but Trent was barely out of the hole. Both went stockstill.

One of the perimeter guards was on the prowl. Wandering off the path patrollers had been pounding all night, he was walking toward a spot between the exit hole and the ferret fence. The goon must have seen or heard something. From where he sat, Langlois could clearly see steam rising from the hole where Bob McBride was waiting on the ladder to crawl out. Could the guard see it, too?

Reavell-Carter watched the guard advance toward the hole with growing apprehension. There were two bodies lying in the snow in front of the guy and it was only a matter of a few more feet before he either saw one or tripped over the other.

The crunch of snow under the German's boots became the squish of slush. He stopped. He noticed the path and the rope. His eyes followed both a few yards to the right and he could make out Shand's body hugging the ground. What he didn't see was Trent lying just two feet to his left.

Slowing unslinging his rifle, the guard brought the stock to his chin and took aim at Shand.

Reavell-Carter had seen enough. Jumping into the open and waving his arms he yelled, *"Nicht schiessen! Nicht schiessen!"* ("Don't shoot! Don't shoot!")

Startled, the guard jerked his weapon up and fired high. Shand sprang to his feet at the sound of the shot and bolted into the woods where he ran past Ogilvie, and Ogilvie took off after him.

The thunderstruck guard fumbled for his flashlight and switched it on. The beam found Reavell-Carter at the edge of the woods walking toward him with his hands up. There was a noise to the right. The guard shined his light that way and flinched when he saw Langlois rise up from behind the ferret fence and surrender, too. But the guard almost jumped out of his skin when he felt a tap on his shoulder and turned to see Trent standing right behind him.

Behind Trent was the tunnel exit. The guard stepped to the edge and pointed his light. There was Bob McBride smiling weakly from the top of a ladder.

The dots finally connected in the guard's brain. He reached for the whistle around the collar of his coat and blew it as loud as he could.

CHAPTER 18

THE COOLER IS FULL

March 26, 1944

THE CRACK OF THE RIFLE SHOT OVER THE north fence was loud enough to wake up Bub Clark in the American compound 400 yards away. The former X-Organization security chief checked his watch and saw it was just before five. He hoped no one had been hit. Then he wondered how many had gotten out.

When he heard the high-pitched shriek of a guard's alert whistle a minute later, Clark knew there was going to be hell to pay.

In Hut 104, none of the stooges by the windows had a

good look at what was going on near Harry's exit hole. The cooler, which sat between the barracks and the north fence, blocked their view. They could, however, see Germans running from the guardhouse at the main gate along the wire and into the woods.

Tunnel boss Crump Ker-Ramsey had shifted the escape into reverse as soon as he heard the rifle go off. First, he told Dave Torrens to have everyone in the barracks destroy their papers and get rid anything else that might tie them to the breakout. Then he hurried down the ladder of the entry shaft to clear the remaining men out of the tunnel before some trigger-happy guard got in there with the machine gun.

Denys Maw, the next man in line at the exit hole after Bob McBride, was standing at the bottom of the exit ladder when he heard the shot. Diving back into the tunnel, he told Joe Moul, the man behind him, and hauler Clive Saxelby that it was time to leave.

Saxelby barreled into Leicester Square where Muckle Muir was waiting for a lift to the exit. Sax made it short and sweet: "The Germans are onto us. Get back to the hut!" He then transferred his trolley to the Piccadilly tracks and took off.

Sax met up with Ormond's stranded trolley halfway to Piccadilly. He explained the change in plans and they worked together, propelling both trolleys the remaining fifty feet back to the changeover. At Piccadilly, Sax and Ormond pulled their carts off the track and leaned them against the walls of the changeover so the men behind them could get by. They then set out for the entry shaft at a rapid crawl.

Out at the exit hole, the guard who stumbled upon the escape motioned with his rifle for McBride to climb out and join Lawrence Reavell-Carter, Roy Langlois, and Len Trent at the ferret fence. By the time Mac ambled over with his hands up, five goons arrived on the run and marched the recaptured POWs off to the guardhouse.

They were held there in temporary custody by two guards, who were more interested in watching the commotion going on outside than keeping an eye on their

German guard in the exit shaft of Harry after the tunnel was discovered

prisoners. That made it very easy for the four RAF officers to toss their false identity cards and other papers into the guardhouse stove.

Nearly 45 minutes later the door burst open and in walked *Kommandant* von Lindeiner, deputy *Kommandant* Simoleit, security chief Broili, and Captain Pieber. The prisoners stood up when they entered. The *Kommandant* was angrier than the prisoners had ever seen him before and his rage only intensified when they declined to answer Pieber's questions about the

171

breakout. Von Lindeiner railed at the treachery of the British to mount an escape when he had treated them so well and warned that for those who got away the revenge of the Gestapo would be swift and brutal.

"You have no idea what you have done," he shouted before ordering the guards to throw the four in the cooler.

One by one the escapers still in the tunnel scrambled back to the entry shaft. Rees was the last one up the ladder. The trap was closed behind him and the red-hot stove placed on top. For the first time Pat Langford was not there to do the honors. He had gotten out with the first group of hard-arsers.

What awaited them in Hut 104 was near chaos. Smoke filled the barracks from more than a dozen little fires in the corridor and some of the rooms where people were burning their papers and maps. Others were eating their road rations and hiding their compasses, German money, and other escape paraphernalia in mattresses and behind false walls.

Two men jumped out of windows on the west side of the hut and raced back to their own barracks. Gunfire from the goonbox nearest the cooler barely missed them and discouraged any copycats.

Down the hall in Room 23, Crump could hear scratching underneath the trap. Did he leave somebody down there? He pulled out Jimmy Davison's checklist to make sure. No, everyone was out. It must be one of the Germans. Let him scratch.

A little after six o'clock the North Compound entrance gates swung open and a convoy of motorcycles and half-tracks thundered into camp and stopped in front of Hut 104. More than seventy soldiers wearing steel helmets and carrying submachine guns jumped out of the trucks and quickly surrounded the barracks. Von Lindeiner followed them through the gate on foot, moving quickly with Simoleit, Broili, and Pieber in his wake. Behind them were Rubberneck and a small army of ferrets.

If anything, the *Kommandant*'s fury was more pronounced entering Hut 104 than it had been leaving the guardhouse. Flecks of spit flew from his mouth as he chewed out the 113 remaining escapers and ordered them outside to be strip-searched. Knowing von Lindeiner to be a decent man with an impossible job, the prisoners took no joy in seeing him so distressed. The escape was going to get him fired, or worse.

It was snowing as the men started coming out and were lined up at gunpoint between huts 104 and 105. Everyone stripped down to his long johns and socks. Ferrets picked through the coats, shirts, pants, and boots and confiscated anything that resembled civilian clothing.

Back inside the hut, Rees and Noble had guessed that the fingers scratching beneath Harry's trap belonged to Charlie Pfelz and let him out. Pfelz was not only the friendliest of all the ferrets, he was also the only German in camp with the courage to explore escape tunnels.

Pfelz was just climbing out of the shaft, flashlight in hand, when von Lindeiner and Rubberneck entered Room 23. Charlie saluted the *Kommandant* and with his customary good cheer described the length and workmanship of the tunnel, pointing out that it even had electric lights. Rubberneck shrank from the *Kommandant's* glare at this last bit of information. Charlie enjoyed the moment. Like most of the ferrets, he hated Rubberneck.

The report on the tunnel had pushed von Lindeiner to the boiling point. He returned outside with his pistol drawn. He didn't intend to shoot anybody, but having it out seemed to calm him down.

Rubberneck had his weapon out, too, only he was looking for an excuse to use it. Coming out of Hut 104 he saw his chance. Rees and Noble, two longtime enemies, were taking their time getting undressed. Holstering his gun, Rubberneck ran over and grabbed each by the collar in an attempt to rip their shirts off. Both spun away and put their fists up in defiance. Instantly, Rubberneck had his pistol out and pointed as Noble's head while one of the guards had his machine gun aimed at Rees.

Luckily for Noble and Rees, von Lindeiner stepped in

and ordered them both to strip immediately. When they had, the *Kommandant* summoned four gun-toting guards and pointed to the shivering kriegies. "Cooler," he said.

Hearing a prisoner behind him mimic the one-word command and another prisoner laugh, von Lindeiner wheeled around and sent them off to the cooler, too. He then waved his pistol at the rest of the assembled prisoners and said, "If there is one more disturbance, I will personally shoot two of you." There was no more trouble.

After the clothing search was finished, the name and face of every man standing in the freezing cold outside Hut 104 was checked against the camp's photo identification card file. They stayed outside for the next two hours while Pieber and his staff went from barracks to barracks conducting a photo check of every prisoner in camp to determine exactly who was missing.

By 8:30 the count was complete. Seventy-six prisoners were unaccounted for and considered to have escaped. The news was a disaster for von Lindeiner, who would now have to inform local authorities and Berlin of the biggest mass escape of the war. He faced a court-martial for sure, not to mention the wrath of the Gestapo.

At nine o'clock, four hours after the escape was discovered, von Lindeiner ordered Pieber to march the would-be escapers outside Hut 104 to the cooler and lock them up for four weeks. When they reached the main gate, however, Pieber was told the cooler was full.

Even jammed with three kriegies to a cell, the cooler couldn't hold more than forty men.

Pieber dismissed the 120 prisoners and they ran back to their individual huts to get warm. Many would never serve their full twenty-eight-day sentences.

CHAPTER 19

ROUNDUP AND REPRISALS

March 25–April 18, 1944

TWO OF THE TELEPHONE CALLS MADE FROM *Kommandant* von Lindeiner's office the morning of the escape were to Lieutenant Colonel Max Wielen, the chief of the Breslau Kripo, or criminal police. Breslau was a hundred miles southeast of Sagan.

The first call, placed to Wielen's home a little after six o'clock, advised him that there had been an escape by an undetermined number of British prisoners. The second, to Wielen's office three hours later, said that seventy-six men had broken out.

Wielen was responsible for coordinating all searches for prisoners gone missing from area POW camps. He reacted to the first call by putting out a *Kriegfahndung,* or general alert. The second call, however, required him to upgrade the emergency to a *Grossfahndung*—"a national hue and cry" and Germany's highest security threat level.

The manhunt would now involve tens of thousands, if not hundreds of thousands, of local and national police, Gestapo, soldiers, civilians, Hitler Youth, and Home Guard among others. Which meant that the escape had achieved its primary goal—to impede the Nazi war effort by tying up as many Germans as possible looking for escaped prisoners.

But for how long could the escaped RAF officers evade capture? And could any of the German-speaking train travelers with the best chances for a home run make it back to England?

Most of the escapers were headed either north to Sweden, west to France, southwest to Switzerland, or south to Czechoslovakia. The train travelers wanted to get out of Germany as quickly as possible so they could avoid the complications of a national dragnet. To do that they needed two things to happen: They had to catch their trains on time and the escape at North Compound couldn't be uncovered by the goons until morning roll-call. In other words, they had to be lucky.

Unfortunately, the escape wasn't blessed with an abundance of good luck.

It got off to a troubling start Friday night when the wood bracing at the top of the exit shaft was found to be frozen solid and the breakout was delayed for over an hour. Then Harry turned out to be fifteen feet short of the woods. Then came the RAF's midnight bombing raid on Berlin, which blacked out Sagan and disrupted train service within a hundred miles of the German capital for almost three hours. And then the escape was discovered at 5 A.M., a good four hours before morning *appell.*

Of the first ten men out of the tunnel, only Roger Bushell, Bernard Scheidhauer, Des Plunkett, and Freddie Dvorak were able to catch a train out of the Sagan railway

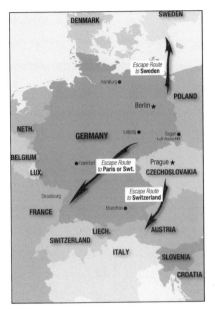

station before midnight. They reached Breslau before they heard about the air raid.

Bushell and Scheidhauer, who were headed to Paris, then took an express from Breslau to Saarbrucken, which was 535 miles west on the French border. Plunkett and Dvorak grabbed a later train to Glatz near the border with Czechoslovakia. Their plan was to link up with friends of Dvorak's in the Czech underground.

Most of the other escapers, however, ran into

181

problems similar to those of Johnny Marshall and Wally Valenta, the first two running mates out of the tunnel.

After making the half-mile walk through the woods from the exit point to the railway station, Marshall and Valenta couldn't find the subway entrance that led to the ticket office and the train platforms above. The X-Organization's directions to the station didn't mention that a shed had recently been built over the entrance to shelter customers from the winter weather. As a result, Johnny and Wally stumbled around in the dark for nearly forty-five minutes looking for a way in.

By the time they finally found their way inside, sirens announcing the approach of the RAF bombers started going off. There were several German guards standing near the ticket office, one of whom ordered the two escapers to get to a bomb shelter.

Dressed as foreign workers with forged transit papers to Prague, Marshall and Valenta were in a difficult position. They had missed their primary train. There was only one other scheduled departure for Czechoslovakia that night and it was certain to be delayed by the air raid.

If the escape was discovered before daylight, any train they were on was certain to be searched. Or, worse yet, they might be caught waiting at the station.

None of those options were appealing, so they decided to leave the station and set out for the Czech border on foot. Valenta, a native Slovak and the X-Organization's intelligence chief, knew the way. With the snow too deep to walk through the woods, they followed the Sagan-to-Breslau autobahn for twelve miles. At dawn on Saturday, less than eight hours after breaking out of North Compound, they ducked into the woods to burrow into the snow and lay low until it got dark again.

At dusk, Wally and Johnny resumed their trek south and were passing through a small village when they ran into three Germans, one of whom was carrying a shotgun. Responding to the *Grossfahndung*, the locals were looking for escaped prisoners. Valenta and Marshall, disheveled and shivering after a day on the lam, tried to bluff their way past the search party, but couldn't. The jig was up.

They were taken to a small jail in Halbau that was

already holding Shorty Armstrong, Hunk Humphreys, and Paul Royle. Early on Sunday the five of them were driven back to Sagan, but instead of being delivered to the cooler at North Compound, they were taken to the less friendly confines of the city jail for interrogation. During the day, fourteen more recaptured escapers were brought in and locked up in the same cell.

Late Monday night all nineteen kriegies were loaded on two trucks and taken forty miles south to Gorlitz. The state-run prison there was a stone fortress with walls three stories high and two feet thick.

Adolf Hitler was first told of the escape late Saturday morning. He was at his mountain retreat near Berchtesgaden in a meeting with Goering, Himmler, and Wehrmacht (armed forces) chief Wilhelm Keitel. Himmler had received a preliminary report from the Kripo office in Breslau and read it aloud.

The war was going badly for the Germans and Hitler was in a terrible mood. The news from Sagan sent him into a towering rage. Calling the seventy-six Allied fliers "air-terrorists" and serious threats to internal security, he demanded that they be hunted down and executed. No interrogations and no mercy. Find them, shoot them all, and cremate their bodies. Teach every prisoner in every German POW camp a lesson they'll never forget.

Goering and Keitel waited until the Fuhrer had calmed down before pointing out that the killings would create an international outcry. The Allies, they said, might retaliate by shooting a like number of German prisoners in their care.

Even Himmler, the architect of the Nazis' civilian death squads and concentration camps, suggested it might not be necessary to kill all the escapers.

"Perhaps half," suggested the slight but sinister head of the criminal and political police.

"Not enough!" snapped Hitler.

"Then fifty, *mein Fuhrer*," said Himmler. "And we'll say they were each shot while trying to escape."

Hitler agreed.

. . .

The following morning, Sunday March 26, Col. Friedrich-Wilhelm von Lindeiner was fired as *Kommandant* of Stalag Luft III. Goering gave the order, sending two Luftwaffe officers to Sagan with an arrest warrant charging von Lindeiner with dereliction of duty.

A few hours after being confined to quarters, the former *Kommandant* heard that some of the escaped prisoners were being held in the Sagan city jail. He called the jail and asked the Gestapo officer in charge to return the prisoners to North Compound. The officer replied that von Lindeiner was no longer in position to give orders, then laughed and hung up.

Three days later, von Lindeiner suffered a mild heart attack. He was allowed to leave camp for his family estate on the edge of town where he was placed under house arrest while awaiting court-martial.

Goering's Luftwaffe and Keitel's Wehrmacht had control over the air force and army prisoner of war camps, but Hitler handed the job of dealing with the Stalag Luft III escapers to Himmler.

Himmler drew up the "Sagan Order" on Monday March 27 and passed it down the security services chain of command. His top deputy, Ernst Kaltenbrenner, a Hitler favorite and the Nazis' chief executioner, gave it to Gestapo boss Heinrich Muller, who in turn handed it to Kripo chief Artur Nebe.

It was left to Nebe to choose the fifty escapers who would be shot. Executions were nothing new for him. Before the war he led one of four major death squads set up to rid the Third Reich of so-called "undesirables." And after the Germans invaded the Soviet Union in 1941, he commanded a larger "liquidation task force" that by his own count killed over 45,000 Russians in five months. More than a few were women and children.

Still, as he sifted through a stack of seventy-six index cards on each escaper, he agonized over who would live or die. For a mass murderer like Nebe, condemning thousands of nameless civilians he had never seen before was easy. Seeing photos and reading brief biographical summaries made the choosing much more difficult. He went through the stack two or three times before deciding which fifty men would be killed. Of the twenty-six who were spared, all were either fathers, husbands, or very young.

The death list was sent out from Berlin to all Gestapo bureaus over secure teletype lines on March 29. The executions were to begin immediately.

By March 29 only a handful of the escapers were still at large. Most had been recaptured within fifty miles of Sagan, but a few came close to getting away.

Wings Day and his Polish running mate Pete Tobolski made it to Berlin and then ninety miles north to Stettin near the Baltic Sea. They found some French POWs working on the docks there who agreed to smuggle them aboard a ship bound for Sweden. One of the Frenchmen, however, turned them in to the Gestapo.

Twelve prisoners were caught in Czechoslovakia. Tim Walenn, Gordon Brettell, Henri Picard, and Rene

Marcinkus were pulled off a train in Schneidemuhl, 130 miles from Danzig. And the quartet of Jimmy Catanach, Arnold Christensen, Halldoe Espelid, and Nils Fugelsang made it 380 miles north to the Danish border before being picked up.

But the cruelest fate awaited Roger Bushell.

Less than thirty-six hours out of North Compound, the mastermind of the Great Escape and his 22-year-old running mate Bernard Scheidhauer were sitting pretty. They had taken two trains and traveled 640 miles west to Saarbrucken, less than nine miles from the border between Germany and France.

After four years of captivity and twelve months supervising the three-tunnel plan to break out of Stalag Luft III, the Big X was on his way to Paris. From there, with help from the French resistance, they could make it to Spain and then to England in less than a week.

Twice he had come close to regaining his freedom and failed. Now, just as it appeared that Bushell's luck was about to change, disaster struck again.

Early in the morning of March 26, he and Scheidhauer

approached a Gestapo checkpoint on the outskirts of Saarbrucken. Posing as two French businessmen headed back to Paris, their papers were in order, their clothes the correct style, and their conversational German impeccable.

They had just been waived through when one of the Gestapo agents wished the unsuspecting Scheidhauer "Good luck" in English.

"Thank you," said Scheidhauer, also in English.

The words were barely out of the Frenchman's mouth when he realized he'd fallen for the trick Bushell had warned all the train travelers about on the eve of the escape. Roger looked at him in disbelief. The agents drew their pistols and marched them off to Gestapo headquarters.

When the "Sagan Order" went out three days later, Bushell and Scheidhauer were both on the condemned list. Roger, in fact, was at the top of the list.

Wasting little time, Saarbrucken Gestapo chief Dr. Leopold Spann asked deputy Emil Schultz to fetch the prisoners while he had their death certificates typed up.

The four men then piled into a Gestapo staff car, and Spann told his driver to head east to Kaiserslautern. He told Bushell and Scheidhauer they were being handed over to civilian authorities.

Twenty-five miles into the trip, Spann ordered the car to stop near a wooded area. The prisoners had their handcuffs removed and were invited to relieve themselves by the side of the road. Spann and Schultz got out with them and as Bushell and Scheidhauer began to unbutton their trousers each was shot in the back of the head.

Their bodies were taken back to Saarbrucken and cremated. Over the next two weeks all across Germany, the Gestapo carried out similar executions of forty-eight more escapers. All the bodies were cremated and the death certificates sent to Berlin.

By April 4, ten days after the breakout, fifteen of the seventy-six escapers had been returned to North Compound. They were all in the cooler, crammed three to a cell.

Thirteen of the fifteen, including Johnny Marshall, Mick Shand, and Keith Ogilvie, had spent a week at the civilian prison in Gorlitz, forty miles south of Sagan. They had been interrogated there by the Gestapo and felt fortunate to be back in camp.

But there had been thirty-five escapers at Gorlitz. Fellow prisoners Wally Valenta, Pat Langford, Al Hake, Ian Cross, and eighteen others had been taken from their cells in ones and twos, put into Gestapo staff cars, and driven off. What happened to them?

On April 6, Senior British Officer Massey was summoned to *Kommandant* Braune's office for an 11 A.M. meeting "of the utmost importance." The new *Kommandant* didn't speak English, so Massey brought Wank Murray along to interpret.

Braune, a fairly tall Luftwaffe colonel of about fifty with thinning hair and a sad face, motioned for the two RAF officers to take a seat while he remained standing behind his desk. He was clearly uncomfortable and had difficulty looking Massey in the eye.

"I am instructed by the German High Command to

inform you," he began, "that forty-one of the escapers were shot while resisting arrest."

Murray leaned forward, not sure he had heard correctly. "How many were shot?" he asked.

"Forty-one," said Braune.

Murray translated for Massey, and the Group Captain fixed a withering gaze on the *Kommandant* before speaking.

"Ask him how many were wounded," Massey said to Murray.

Braune replied that he had been instructed to read the statement only and not answer any questions.

Massey to Murray: "Ask him again."

"I think none were wounded," said Braune.

"None wounded?" said Massey, making no attempt to hide his anger. "Do you mean to tell me that forty-one men were shot while supposedly resisting arrest and they were all killed?"

Braune looked down at the document on his desk. "I regret I can only read to you what is in this communiqué."

"I want to see a of list names," said Massey.

"I do not have that information," said Braune.

Massey was insistent. "I expect a complete list of who was shot and what happened to the bodies, so we can arrange for burial and the disposal of their effects."

"Of course," said Braune.

Hans Pieber, who ushered Massey and Murray back to North Compound, was ashen faced. "This is such a terrible thing," he said. "You must believe the Luftwaffe was not involved in any way."

Massey called the senior officers to a special meeting at the camp theater that afternoon and told them about the killings. The compound went numb with the news. Whose names were on the list?

Late in the afternoon on April 15 the names of the dead were posted. There were forty-seven names on the list, not forty-one. A few days later three more names were added, making it an even fifty.

THE BEGINNING OF THE END OF WORLD War II in Europe came shortly after dawn on D-Day, June 6, 1944. Catching the Germans by surprise on the northern coast of France, the Allies landed 154,000 troops along a sixty-mile stretch of Normandy beachfront guarded by heavily fortified cliffs. It was the greatest seaborne invasion in military history.

At Stalag Luft III, a letter from England arrived at North Compound in mid-June that cheered up the prisoners as much as the news of the invasion. Using code names agreed to before the escape, Jens Muller and Per Bergsland wrote to say they had made it home safely.

The two Norwegians had reached Stettin by train the

night after the breakout and contacted a couple of Swedish sailors near the harbor. They were smuggled onto an outbound ship on March 29 and reached Stockholm the following day. Sweden was a neutral country in the war, so they simply reported to the British consulate and were back in London within a few days.

In July another letter reached camp, this one from Dutchman Bob van der Stok. He also had managed a home run but only after being at large for three months. His one-man odyssey had taken him from Sagan, south to Breslau, north to Holland, then to Belgium, Spain, and British-held Gibraltar before he was flown back to England in June.

Added to the fifteen men returned to North Compound and the fifty who were executed, those three brought the number of escapers accounted for to sixty-eight. There was still no word on the whereabouts of eight men—Wings Day, Johnny Dodge, Sydney Dowse, Jimmy James, Raymond van Wymeersch, Des Plunkett, Ivo Tonder, and Freddie Dvorak.

They were behind bars. Plunkett and Czechs Tonder

and Dvorak were being held in a Czechoslovakian prison west of Prague, while Wings, Dodge, Dowse, James, and van Wymeersch had been sent to Sachsenhausen concentration camp north of Berlin. Although several of them were subjected to brutal interrogations by the Gestapo, all eight men would survive the remaining ten months of the war in Europe.

Former Stalag Luft III *Kommandant* von Lindeiner was court-martialed on October 5 and sentenced to a year in a military prison.

While preparing for the trial, von Lindeiner learned that urns and boxes containing the ashes of the fifty escapers executed by the Gestapo had been returned to Sagan. He also heard that the remaining prisoners of North Compound wanted to build a memorial to the fifty at a little cemetery near camp. Von Lindeiner felt it was his duty as an officer and a gentleman to pay tribute to the men, so he donated the materials needed to build the memorial.

On December 4, a fifteen-minute funeral service was

held at the cemetery. Thirty RAF officers were allowed to attend. A wreath was laid, an honor guard of prison camp riflemen fired a salute to the dead, and a trumpeter from the North Compound orchestra played "Last Post."

The war entered its last few months in 1945. Allied forces were closing in on Berlin from all sides and the Germans were getting desperate. In February, Johnny Dodge was taken from his cell at Sachsenhausen to meet Hitler's interpreter, Dr. Paul Schmidt.

"You are going home, my dear Mr. Dodge," said Dr. Schmidt. "When you get there, I imagine you will meet your kinsman Mr. Churchill. I would like you to tell him that the Allies' demand of 'unconditional surrender' is out of the question. Surrender, yes. Unconditional, no."

As a relative of British Prime Minister Winston Churchill, Dodge was being asked to forget what he'd been through the last five years and help the Germans get a favorable peace deal. Ridiculous.

The Dodger was handed over to a member of the German Foreign Ministry who had orders to take him to the Swiss border. On the way they were almost incinerated in an Allied bombing raid on Dresden, bombed out again in Weimar, and arrested as spies and later released in Regensburg. By the time they finally reached Switzerland it was April 25.

Hitler killed himself on April 30.

Dodge made it back to London the first week in May. On May 5, the 50-year-old American-born British Major was invited to dinner with the 69-year-old Prime Minister at 10 Downing Street. Afterwards, over cigars and brandy, Johnny regaled Churchill with tales of prison camp life and the Great Escape from Stalag Luft III.

Two days later, the Germans surrendered unconditionally and the war was over.

After the war, however, there would be consequences for those members of the Gestapo who were involved in the murders of the fifty escapers. British officers conducted an investigation and brought twenty-one Gestapo officers to trial. All but one were convicted and fourteen of them were hanged.

. . .

The Great Escape has endured as one of the most remarkable stories of World War II because the men who carried it off never, never gave in. It is also that rare war story where the high-spirited heroes had no guns. As prisoners of war, their only weapons were their wits, their willpower, and their faith in each other.

The enemy appeared to have every advantage.

Except the urge to be free.

This list contains the names of the Allied flying officers who broke out of North Compound at Stalag Luft III on the night of March 24–25, 1944. Note that (+) indicates the 50 prisoners who were murdered by the Germans; their ages are also given. Countries of foreign officers who flew for the RAF are in parenthesis.

Royal Air Force (Britain)

Flight Lieutenant Albert (Shorty) Armstrong

Sergeant Per Bergsland, a/k/a/ Peter Rockland (Norway)

Flight Lieutenant Tony Bethell

+Flight Lieutenant Gordon Brettell, 29

Flight Lieutenant Les Brodrick

+Flight Lieutenant Johnny Bull, 27

+Squadron Leader Roger Bushell, 33

+Flight Lieutenant Mike Casey, 26

Flight Lieutenant Dick Churchill

+Flying Officer Dennis Cochran, 22

+Squadron Leader Ian Cross, 25

Wing Commander Harry (Wings) Day

Major Johnny Dodge (Territorial Army)

Flight Lieutenant Sydney Dowse

Flight Lieutenant Freddie Dvorak (Czechoslovakia)

+Flight Lieutenant Brian Evans, 24

Flight Lieutenant Bernard (Pop) Green

+Flight Lieutenant Jack Grisman, 29

+Flight Lieutenant Sandy Gunn, 24

+Flight Lieutenant Chaz Hall, 25

+Flight Lieutenant Tony Hayter, 23

+Flight Lieutenant Edgar (Hunk) Humphreys, 29

Pilot Officer Jimmy James

+Flight Lieutenant Tony Kiewnarski (Poland), 45

+Squadron Leader Tom Kirby-Green, 26

+Flying Officer Adam Kolanowski (Poland), 30

+Flying Officer Stanislaw (Danny) Krol (Poland), 28

Flight Lieutenant Roy Langlois

+Flight Lieutenant Tom Leigh, 29

+Flight Lieutenant Les (Cookie) Long, 29

+Flight Lieutenant René Marcinkus (Lithuania), 33

Flight Lieutenant Johnny Marshall

Flight Lieutenant A.T. McDonald

+Flight Lieutenant Harold Milford, 29

+Flying Officer Jerzy Mondschein (Poland), 35

Second Lieutenant Jens Muller (Norway)

Flight Lieutenant Bob Nelson

Flight Lieutenant Keith Ogilvie

+Flying Officer Kaz Pawluk (Poland), 37

+Flight Lieutenant Henri Picard (Belgium), 27

Flight Lieutenant Des Plunkett

Squadron Leader Lawrence Reavell-Carter

Pilot Officer Paul Royle

+Flying Officer Bob Stewart, 32

+Flying Officer Johnny Stower (Argentina), 27

+Flying Officer Denys Street, 22

+Flight Lieutenant Cyril Swain, 32

+Flying Officer Peter Tobolski (Poland), 38

Flight Lieutenant Ivo Tonder (Czechoslovakia)

+Flight Lieutenant Arnost (Wally) Valenta
(Czechoslovakia), 31

Flight Lieutenant Bob van der Stok (Holland)

Flight Lieutenant Raymond van Wymeersch (France)

+Flight Lieutenant Tim Walenn, 27

+Flight Lieutenant John Williams, 26

Royal Navy (Britain)

Lieutenant Des Neely

Lieutenant Doug Poynter

Royal Canadian Air Force

+Flying Officer Hank Birkland, 26

Flight Lieutenant Bill Cameron

+Flying Officer Gordon Kidder, 29

+Flight Lieutenant Pat Langford, 24

+Flight Lieutenant George McGill, 25

Flight Lieutenant Alfred (Tommy) Thompson

+Flight Lieutenant Jimmy Wernham, 27

+Flight Lieutenant George Wiley, 22

Royal Australian Air Force

+Squadron Leader Jimmy Catanach, 22

+Flight Lieutenant Al Hake, 27

+Flight Lieutenant Reg (Rusty) Kierath, 29

+Squadron Leader John (Willy) Williams, 24

Royal New Zealand Air Force

+Flying Officer Arnold Christensen, 21

+Flying Officer Porokoru (Johnny) Pohe, 29

Flight Lieutenant Mick Shand

Squadron Leader Len Trent

Royal Norwegian Air Force

+Sergeant Halldor Espelid, 23

+Lieutenant Nils Fugelsang, 25

Royal South African Air Force

+Lieutenant Johannes Gouws, 24

+Lieutenant Neville McGarr, 26

+Lieutenant Rupert (John) Stevens, 25

Free French Air Force

+Lieutenant Bernard Scheidhauer, 22

Royal Hellenic Air Force (Greece)

+Pilot Officer Sotiris (Nick) Skanziklas, 22

BIBLIOGRAPHY

One way to measure the significance of an event is by the number of excellent books written about it. I have used the following accounts of "The Great Escape," by participants and historians, in the course of my research:

Escape from Germany: The Methods of Escape Used by RAF Airmen During the Second World War, by Aiden Crawley, Her Majesty's Stationery Office, London, 1987

A Gallant Company: The True Story of "The Great Escape," by Jonathan F. Vance, ibooks, New York, 2000

The Great Escape, by Paul Brickhill, Ballantine Books, New York, 1983

The Great Escape from Stalag Luft III: The Full Story of How 76 Allied Officers Carried Out World War II's Most Remarkable Mass Escape, by Tim Carroll, Pocket Books, New York, 2004

Lie in the Dark and Listen: The Remarkable Exploits of a WWII Bomber Pilot and Great Escaper, by Ken Rees with Karen Arrandale, Grub Street, London, 2004

Lonesome Road, by George Harsh, W.W. Norton & Co., New York, 1971

The Longest Tunnel: The True Story of World War II's Great Escape, by Alan Burgess, Bluejacket Books, Annapolis, Md., 2004

Moonless Night: One Man's Struggle for Freedom, 1940–45, by B.A. (Jimmy) James, Ivy Books, New York, 1983

Sage: The Man the Nazi's Couldn't Hold, by Jerry Sage, Dell, New York, 1985

Stalag Luft III: The Secret Story of "The Great Escape," by Arthur A. Durand, Touchstone, New York, 1989

33 Months as a POW in Stalag Luft III: A World War II

Airman Tells His Story, by Albert P. (Bub) Clark, Fulcrum Publishing, Golden, Colo., 2004

Wings Day: The Man Who Led the RAF's Epic Battle in German Captivity, by Sydney Smith, Pan Books Ltd., London, 1968

The Wooden Horse, by Eric Williams, Bantam Books, New York, 1951

Series

The Epic of Flight

Knights of the Air, by Ezra Bowen, Time-Life Books, Alexandria, Va., 1980

World War II

The Air War in Europe, by Ronald H. Bailey, Time-Life Books, Alexandria, Va., 1987

The Battle of Britain, by Leonard Mosley, Time-Life Books, Alexandria, Va., 1989

Prisoners of War, by Ronald H. Bailey, Time-Life Books, Alexandria, Va., 1983

INDEX

Note: Page numbers in *italics* refer to illustrations.

American Eagle Squadron, 11

Armstrong, Albert "Shorty," 184

Battle of Britain, 1–2

Battle of Dunkirk, 17

BBC, 94

Bergsland, Per, 195–96

Birkland, Hank, 57, 68, 161

Blitz, 3

Braune, *Kommandant,* 192–94

Brettell, Gordon, 145, 188

Broili, Adolf, 70, 82, 83, 122, 171, 173

Buckley, Jimmy, 11–12, 15, 16, 19

Bull, Johnny, 20, 73, 127–29, 150–53, 154–57

Bushell, Roger, 11–12, *17,* 100, 129

as "Big X," 16, 19, 50, 67, 69, 74, 90–91, 102

and changes in plans, 90–91, 102, 119, 121, 131

early years of, 16–17

and the escape, 154–55, 157, 162, 180–81

and escape committee, 20, 102–4, 143

Bushell, Roger (*cont.*)
and escape procedures,
134, 136–37, 140, 143–44,
146–47, 149
on escape roster, 118
execution of, 191, 202
and Fourth of July, 62,
63–64
and Gestapo practices,
132–33, 141
original capture of, 18
pep talk by, 88–89
recapture of, 189–91
as theater player, 91,
122–23, 143
and Tom's discovery, 83,
88
tunnel plans of, 20, 28–29,
47, 59, 77, 92

Canton, Conk, 42, 103, 114,
145, 150
Casey, Mike, 83–84

Cassie, Alex, 144–45
Catanach, Jimmy, 189
Christensen, Arnold,
189
Christmas Revue, 100
Churchill, Winston, 1–2, 15,
198–99
Clark, Bub:
and diversions, 31, 90
and the escape, 146–47,
168
and security, 20, 36, 47, 49,
68, 72
Cornish, Geoff, 56
Cross, Ian, 106, 107, 192

Davison, Jimmy, 152, 158
Day, Harry "Wings":
background of, 6–7
cover story of, 137, 149
earlier escape attempts by,
7
escape of, 159–60, 196

and Fourth of July, 63

and handbook theft, 99

recapture of, 188, 197

and reopening Harry, 103

teamwork promoted by,
7–8, 106

and Tom's discovery, 83

transfers of, 15, 16, 19, 28

D-Day, 195

Dean & Dawson, forged
documents by, 119, 135,
144

Dick (tunnel):

air pumps for, 49, 51

construction materials for,
26, 41–42

digging the shaft for, 40

fat lamps in, 52, 53

plans for, 20–22, 28–29

sand stored in, 72, 73, 75,
92, 104

temporary closing of, 59,
88

trapdoor of, 30

as workshop and storage
area, 92, 96, 119, 129,
136

Dodge, John Bigelow "Artful
Dodger":

and Churchill, 15,
198–99

escape attempts of, 15

in prison, 196, 197

and singing club, 32, 50,
63

transfers of, 15, 28

Dowse, Sydney, 151, 157, 160,
196, 197

Dvorak, Freddie, 180–81,
196–97

East Compound, 28

tunnels underneath, 37,
43, 54

Ellis, John, 143

Espelid, Halldor, 189

Fanshawe, Hornblower:
  and reopening Harry,
    103
  and sand dispersal, 43–46,
    60, 72, 77, 103, 104,
    124–25
  transfer of, 122, 124
ferrets (nosy German
    guards), 5, 27, 49–50,
    68–69, 75, 118, 174
Floody, Wally:
  cave-ins on, 42, 60,
    114–15
  and finishing Harry,
    119–20
  original capture of, 37
  and reopening Harry, 103,
    108, 114
  transfer of, 122, 124
  as tunnel boss, 20, 36–37,
    41, 60, 69
  tunnel plans of, 28, 43, 51,
    54, 77–78

Fourth of July celebration,
    60–64
France, surrender in World
    War II, 1
Fugelsang, Nils, 189

Geneva Convention, 5–6,
    132
Germany:
  air raids against cities in, 3,
    158–59, 180
  Gestapo (security police),
    see Gestapo
  Great Britain attacked by,
    1–2, 3
  Kripo (criminal police) of,
    85, 178
  Luftwaffe (air force), 2–3,
    86, 186
  Reich Security Office,
    85
  Soviet Union invaded by,
    187–88

SS (political police) of,
85

surrender of, 199

Third Reich death squads,
187

war defeats of, 184, 198

war victories of, 1

Gestapo (security police):

dealing with escapees, 85,
132–33, 172, 190–91,
192–94, 197

prisoners executed by, 133,
185, 187–88, 191, 193–94,
199

and Stalag security,
84–85

trick used by, 141, 190

Glemnitz, Hermann, 43

and earlier escape
attempts, 26–27

and prisoner transfers, 91

security moves by, 68–70,
74, 76–77

and Tom's discovery, 82,
83

tunneling suspected by,
65–72, 78–79

Goering, Hermann, 8–9, 86,
184–85, 186

goons (German guards), 5

goon tamers, 67

Great Britain:

Battle of Britain, 1–2

and the Blitz, 3

Griese, Karl "Rubberneck,"
27

and foiled escape, 173,
174–75

on leave, 119–20, 125

searches for tunnels,
68, 70–71, 78, 111–12,
119, 120, 130, 134

and tightened security,
91–92, 121–23

and Tom's discovery, 82,
84, 85

Griffith, Billy, 148

Guest, Tommy, 22, 137, 149

Hake, Al, 22, 138, 144, 192

Hall, Len, 143

Harry (tunnel):

  air pumps for, 49, 51, 108–9

  as back-up tunnel, 75

  changeover stops in, 104, 110, 115, 151, 158, 159

  completion of, 120, 125, 129, 135

  construction materials for, 26, 41–42

  detail of, 38–39

  digging of, 31, 40, 109, 120, 125

  escape foiled, 165–67, 168–74, 171

  the escape from, 150–53, 154–65

  exit shaft for, 126–30, 153, 171

  final preparations in, 145, 146

  length of, 103–4, 110, 114, 115–16, 125–26, 180

  lights in, 52, 53, 96, 109, 145, 159, 161

  plans for, 20–22, 28–32, 92, 102–3

  reopening of, 92, 96, 102–4, 108–9, 114, 145

  surveying of, 115–16, 130

  temporary closing of, 59, 88

  trapdoor for, 30–31, 110–11, 130, 135

Harsh, George:

  as convicted murderer, 34–36

  and Fourth of July, 62

  as hospital orderly, 35–36

original capture of, 36

transfer of, 122, 124

and tunnel security,
36–37, 67, 68, 90, 103,
112, 120

Herman (ferret), 80

Himmler, Heinrich, 85–86,
184–85, 187

Hitler, Adolf, 1, 9, 184–85, 187,
199

Humphreys, Edgar "Hunk,"
184

James, Jimmy, 106, 107, 144,
196, 197

Jennens, Bill, 131–32, 133

Jones, Davy, 60

Kaltenbrenner, Ernst,
187

Keitel, Wilhelm, 184–85

Ker-Ramsey, Crump, 20, 42,
57, 73, 84

and escape foiled, 169

and escape procedures,
142, 145, 150, 152,
157–60, 163, 164

and Harry's exit shaft, 127,
129

and reopening Harry, 103,
108, 114, 145

as tunnel boss, 124, 125, 145

Kirby-Green, Tom, 103, 161

kriegie brew, 61, 63, 100

kriegies, 4, 96–100

Krol, Danny, 128

Lamond, Piglet, 56

Langford, Pat:
and the escape, 145,
172

and evacuation plans,
120

and Harry's trapdoor,
108, 110, 112–13, 130,
135, 172

Langford, Pat (*cont.*)
  recapture of, 192
  and reopening Harry,
    108, 110, 145
  and tunnel completion,
    129
Langlois, Roy, 164–65, 167,
  170
Lindeiner, Friedrich von, *12*,
  91, 100
  and cooperation, 22,
    59
  and escape aftermath,
    178, 186, 197
  and escape plans,
    132–33
  and foiled escape, 171–72,
    173–77
  and Gestapo orders,
    132–33
  and other escape
    attempts, 13,
    14–15

  respectful treatment of
    prisoners by, 13, 22,
    93–94, 95, 131–32, 172,
    197
  and thefts from limousine,
    98–99
  and Tom's discovery,
    82–83, 84, 85
Lubbock, Eric, 139–40

Marcinkus, René, 188–89
Marshall, Johnny:
  digging the tunnel, 127
  and the escape, 118,
    150, 152, 154–55,
    157, 182
  recapture of, 183, 192
  and tunnel plans, 20
Massey, Herbert, 16, 22, 59,
  110, 149, 192–94
Mauthausen Concentration
  Camp, 133
Maw, Denys, 169

McBride, Bob, 165, 167, 169, 170

McGill, George, 103, 124, 144

McIntosh, Digger, 49

Minskewitz (pilot), 29–31, 68, 77

Moul, Joe, 169

Muir, Muckle, 169

Muller, Heinrich, 187

Muller, Jens, 195–96

Murray, Wank, 192, 194

Nebe, Artur, 187

Nelson, Bob, 55

Nichols, Nick, 11–13

Noble, Red, 95–96, 109, 127, 129, 147, 174, 175

North Compound, 19–20 bunk rooms, 24–26, 25 construction of, 22–26

escape tunnels in, see Dick; Harry; Tom

and foiled escape, 173–77

huts, 24–25

prisoners returned to, 191–92, 196–97

public address system for, 95–96

stoves, 108

Ogilvie, Keith, 165, 166, 192

Pfelz, Karl "Charlie," 82, 174–75

Picard, Henri, 188

Pieber, Hans, 43, 77, 83 and foiled escape, 171, 173, 177, 194 and roll calls, 63, 64, 69, 119

Plunkett, Des, 22, 138–39, 180–81, 196–97

prisoners of war:

  choosing escapees,
    116–18

  cover stories of, 135,
    136–37

  diversions by, 31–32,
    93–94

  the escape, 150–53, 154–67,
    199, 200

  escape as duty of, 7, 13,
    106

  escape procedures,
    134–50

  escape routes, 181

  executions of, 133, 185,
    187–88, 191, 193–94, 197,
    199

  Geneva Convention
    protection of, 5–6, 132

  Gestapo treatment of, 85,
    132–33, 172, 190–91,
    192–94, 197

  home runs of, 7, 195–96

  hooligans, 45, 46

  jurisdiction over,
    186–87

  as kriegies, 4, 31

  list of escapers, 201–6

  memorials to, 197–98

  in military camps,
    85–86

  morale of, 7–8, 94, 106

  parole system honored by,
    97

  penguins, 46, 66, 75

  RAF in Stalag Luft I, 4

  recaptured, 179–84, 185,
    188–92

  roll calls (appells) of, 52,
    63, 64, 69, 119, 120–21

  roughnecks, 45–46

  singing clubs of, 32, 50–51,
    63

  as stooges, 31, 49–50, 92

  teamwork of, 7–8, 106,
    116

RAF (Royal Air Force):
  against German Luftwaffe,
    2–3
  American Eagle Squadron,
    11
  captured, see prisoners of
    war
  downed flight crews of,
    3–4
  duty pilots in, 47
  officer's duty to escape, 7,
    13, 106
  raids against German
    cities, 3, 158–59, 180
Reavell-Carter, Lawrence,
  164–66, 170
Red Cross parcel boxes:
  Christmas parcels, 100
  DP alert signals with, 48
  empty, 78
  Klim powdered milk in,
    52
  news from home in, 94

storing sand in, 76–77
tin cans in, 51–52
Rees, Shag, 147, 172, 174, 175
Royle, Paul, 184
Rubberneck, see Griese, Karl

Sage, Jerry, 28
  and Fourth of July, 60, 62,
    63
  and hooligans, 45, 46
  and sand dispersal, 75, 78,
    106
  and singing clubs, 32, 50
sand, 27
  dangers of, 40–41, 114–15
  diggers in, 53–57
  dumping grounds for,
    45–46, 75
  in exit shaft, 126–30
  German discoveries of, 67,
    118–19
  getting rid of, 43–46, 104
  in Red Cross boxes, 51–52

sand (*cont.*)

  systems for moving, 45–46, 54–57

  trolleys for transport of, 54–55

  in trouser bags, 44–45, 46, 66

  and tunnel cave-ins, 42–43, 53, 60, 114, 161

  under the theater, 104–7

Saxelby, Clive, 169–70

Scheidhauer, Bernard, 136, 157, 180–81, 189–91

Schmidt, Paul, 198

Schultz, Emil, 190–91

Shand, Mick, 165, 166, 192

"Silent Night," 101

Simoleit, *Kommandant*, 171, 173

South Compound:

  American prisoners moved to, 89–90

construction of, 58–59, 69, 77, 89

Soviet Union, German invasion of, 187–88

Spann, Leopold, 190–91

Stalag Luft I (Air Force Prison Camp I), 4–6

  escape attempts from, 5

  sand underneath, see sand

  security in, 5

  terms used in, 5

  tunnels dug underneath, 6, 69

  X-Organization formed at, 8

Stalag Luft III (Air Force Prison Camp III):

  Christmas in, 100–101

  duty pilots (DPs) in, 47–48

  escape attempts from, 14, 26, 37, 94, 125

  escape foiled in, 168–74

escape plans, see
X-Organization

as escape proof, 9–11, 14

escape tunnels in, see
Dick; Harry; Tom

Fourth of July celebration
in, 60–64

full moon over, 113, 114

gardens of, 46, 67, 75

German suspicions in,
65–72

Gestapo criticism of,
84–85

Hut 110 library, 48–49

layout of, 9–11

microphones underground
in, 10–11, 66

North Compound, see
North Compound

theater of, 91, 93–94, 97,
100, 105–6

Toft and Nichols' escape
from, 11–13

visiting general's
limousine at, 97–100

Staubo, Jean, 150

Stevens, Rupert (John), 157

Tobolski, Peter, 137, 149, 188

Toft, Ken, 11–13

Tom (tunnel):
accelerated work on,
59–60, 69, 73

air pumps for, 49, 51

construction materials for,
26, 41–42

demolition of, 83, 86–87

digging the shaft for, 31,
40

fat lamps in, 52, 53

German discovery of, 80,
81–86, 88, 102

length of, 74–75, 77, 82

plans for, 20–22, 28–32

temporary closing of, 72

trapdoor for, 29–30, 68, 80

Tonder, Ivo, 196–97

Torrens, David, 148–49, 164, 169

Travis, Johnny, 22, 30, 48–50, 55, 92, 106, 126–27, 139

Trent, Len, 165, 166, 167, 170

Tuck, Bob, 118, 122, 136

Tyrie, Jim, 122

U.S. Army Air Force, 3

Valenta, Wally:
    and the escape, 118, 157, 182
    German contact team of, 67, 78, 90, 119
    recapture of, 183, 192

van der Stok, Bob, 196

van Wymeersch, Raymond, 196, 197

Walenn, Tim, 22, 99, 119, 135, 136, 144, 188

Walter (German contact), 119

Webster, George, 90

Weir, Scruffy, 57

Wielen, Max, 178–79

Williams, John "Willy," 41

World War I, 6–7

World War II:
    Allied victories in, 94
    end of, 195, 198, 199
    German surrender in, 199
    German victories in, 1

X-Organization:
    and changes of plans, 88–91, 130, 156–57
    command of ("Big X"), 12, 16, 19
    and construction of North Compound, 22–26
    duty pilots (DPs) for, 47–48
    erasing the evidence, 169, 171, 172

escape committee

members, 20, 22, 103, 143

and escape foiled, 168–74

escape support factories of, 22, 92, 135, 137–40, 147

forged documents of, 12, 22, 92, 93, 117, 119, 135–36, 144–45, 146, 155

initial plans of, 20–22

layout of, 23–26

sign-up sheets for, 33

tailoring department of, 22, 137–38, 149

teamwork of, 8, 41, 106, 116, 124

and Toft and Nichols' escape, 11–12

tools acquired by, 48–50

Zillessen, Axel, 139

ABOUT THE AUTHOR

Mike Meserole is an author and editor who began his career with *The Berkshire Eagle* in Pittsfield, Massachusetts. He joined fledgling cable television sports network ESPN in 1981, created the *Information Please Sports Almanac* (now *ESPN Sports Almanac*) in 1989, and wrote *20th Century Sports: Images of Greatness* for *Sports Illustrated* in 1999. He currently produces an annual sports desk calendar. His interest in World War II began at a young age with the discovery of *LIFE's Picture History of World War II* in the family living room bookcase.

BOOKS IN THIS SERIES

Abraham Lincoln: Friend of the People
BY CLARA INGRAM JUDSON

Admiral Richard Byrd: Alone in the Antarctic
BY PAUL RINK

Alexander the Great
BY JOHN GUNTHER

Amelia Earhart: Flying Solo
BY JOHN BURKE

The Barbary Pirates
BY C. S. FORESTER

Battle in the Arctic Seas
BY THEODORE TAYLOR

Behind Enemy Lines: A Young Pilot's Story
BY H. R. DEMALLIE

Ben Franklin: Inventing America
BY THOMAS FLEMING

Danger in the Desert: True Adventures of a Dinosaur Hunter
BY ROGER COHEN

Daniel Boone: The Opening of the Wilderness
BY JOHN MASON BROWN

General George Patton: Old Blood and Guts
BY ALDEN HATCH

George Washington: Frontier Colonel
BY STERLING NORTH

Geronimo: Wolf of the Warpath
BY RALPH MOODY

The Great Escape: The Longest Tunnel
BY MIKE MESEROLE

Invasion: The Story of D-Day
BY BRUCE BLIVEN, JR.

Jamestown: The Perilous Adventure
BY OLGA HALL-QUEST

Joan of Arc: Warrior Saint
BY JAY WILLIAMS

John Paul Jones: The Pirate Patriot
BY ARMSTRONG SPERRY

Lawrence of Arabia
BY ALISTAIR MACLEAN

Lee and Grant at Appomattox
BY MACKINLAY KANTOR

Path to the Pacific: The Story of Sacagawea
BY NETA LOHNES FRAZIER

Pearl Harbor Attack
BY EDWIN P. HOYT

The Sinking of the Bismarck: The Deadly Hunt
BY WILLIAM SHIRER

Stampede for Gold: The Story of the Klondike Rush
BY PIERRE BERTON

The Stouthearted Seven: Orphaned on the Oregon Trail
BY NETA LOHNES FRAZIER

Swamp Fox of the Revolution
BY STEWART H. HOLBROOK

Teddy Roosevelt: An American Rough Rider
BY JOHN A. GARRATY

✳STERLING POINT BOOKS